Disney • PIXAR

TOY STORY

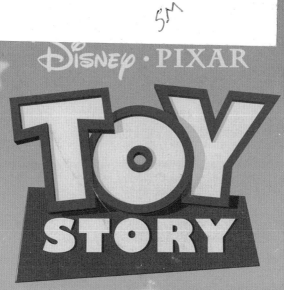

ROSS RICHIE
chief executive officer

ANDREW COSBY
chief creative officer

MARK WAID
editor-in-chief

ADAM FORTIER
vice president,
publishing

CHIP MOSHER
marketing director

MATT GAGNON
managing editor

TOY STORY: MYSTERIOUS STRANGER – July 2009 published by BOOM! KIDS, a division of Boom
Entertainment, Inc. All contents © 2009 Disney Enterprises, Inc. All rights reserved. Slinky ® Dog is a registered
trademark of Poof-Slinky, Inc. © Poof-Slinky, Inc. Etch A Sketch ® © The Ohio Art Company. BOOM! KIDS and the
BOOM! KIDS logo are trademarks of Boom Entertainment, Inc., registered in various countries and categories.
All rights reserved. Office of publication: 6310 San Vicente Blvd Ste 404, Los Angeles, CA 90048. Printed in
Canada.

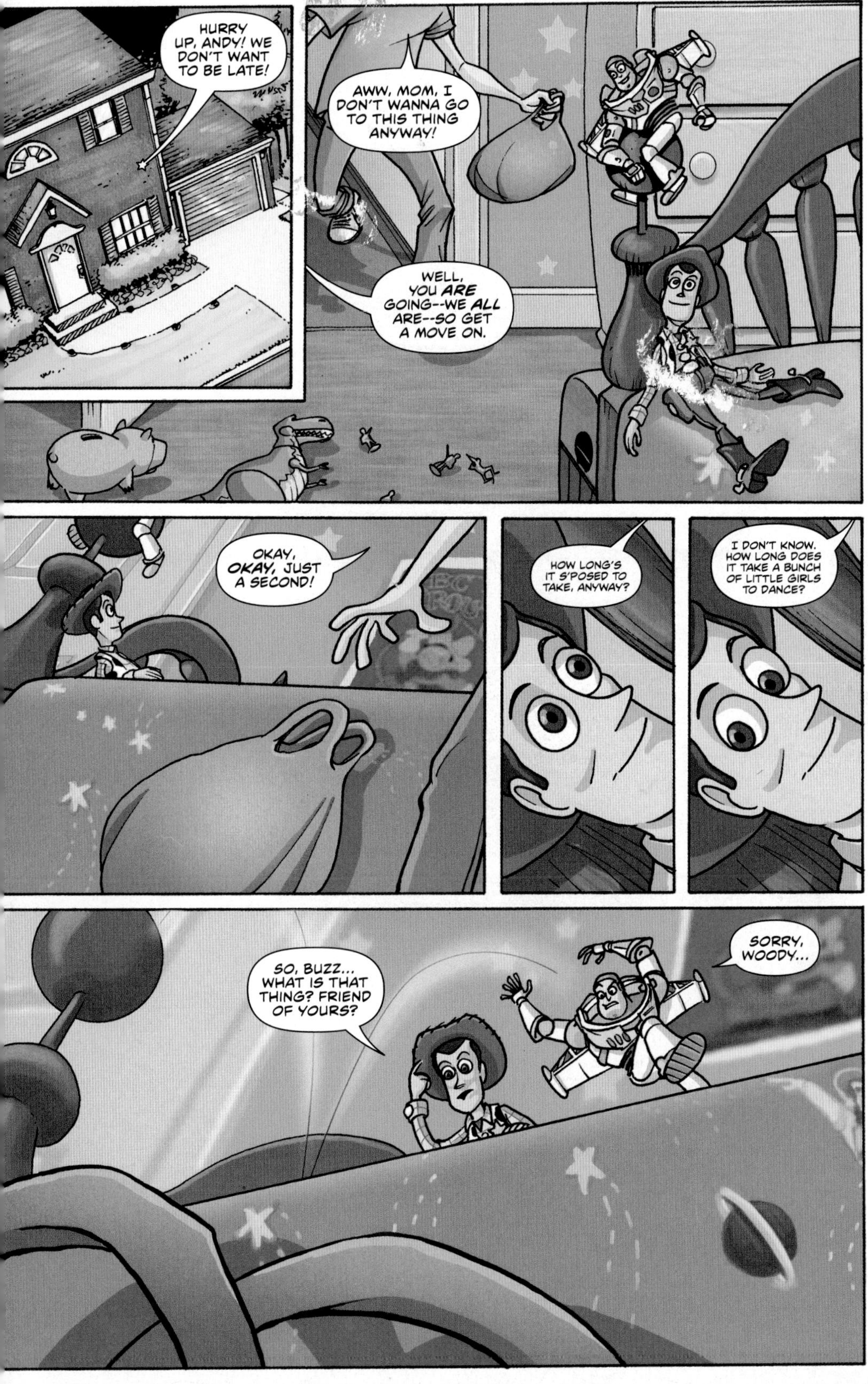
HURRY UP, ANDY! WE DON'T WANT TO BE LATE!
AWW, MOM, I DON'T WANNA GO TO THIS THING ANYWAY!
WELL, YOU ARE GOING--WE ALL ARE--SO GET A MOVE ON.
OKAY, OKAY, JUST A SECOND!
HOW LONG'S IT S'POSED TO TAKE, ANYWAY?
I DON'T KNOW. HOW LONG DOES IT TAKE A BUNCH OF LITTLE GIRLS TO DANCE?
SO, BUZZ... WHAT IS THAT THING? FRIEND OF YOURS?
SORRY, WOODY...

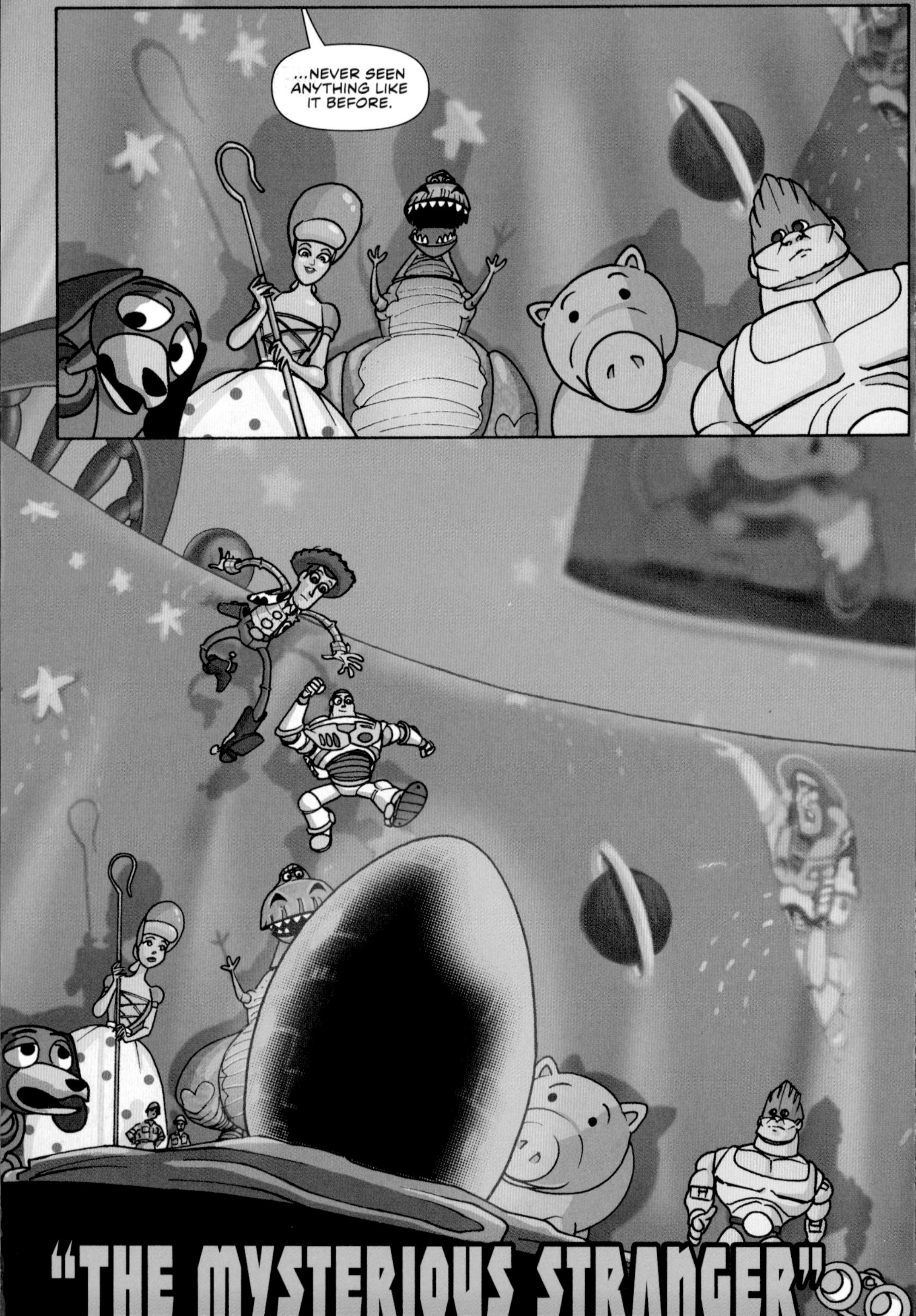
...NEVER SEEN ANYTHING LIKE IT BEFORE.

"THE MYSTERIOUS STRANGER"

Written by Dan Jolley • Illustrated by Chris Moreno • Colored by Veronica Gandini
Lettered by Deron Bennett • Edited by Paul Morrissey

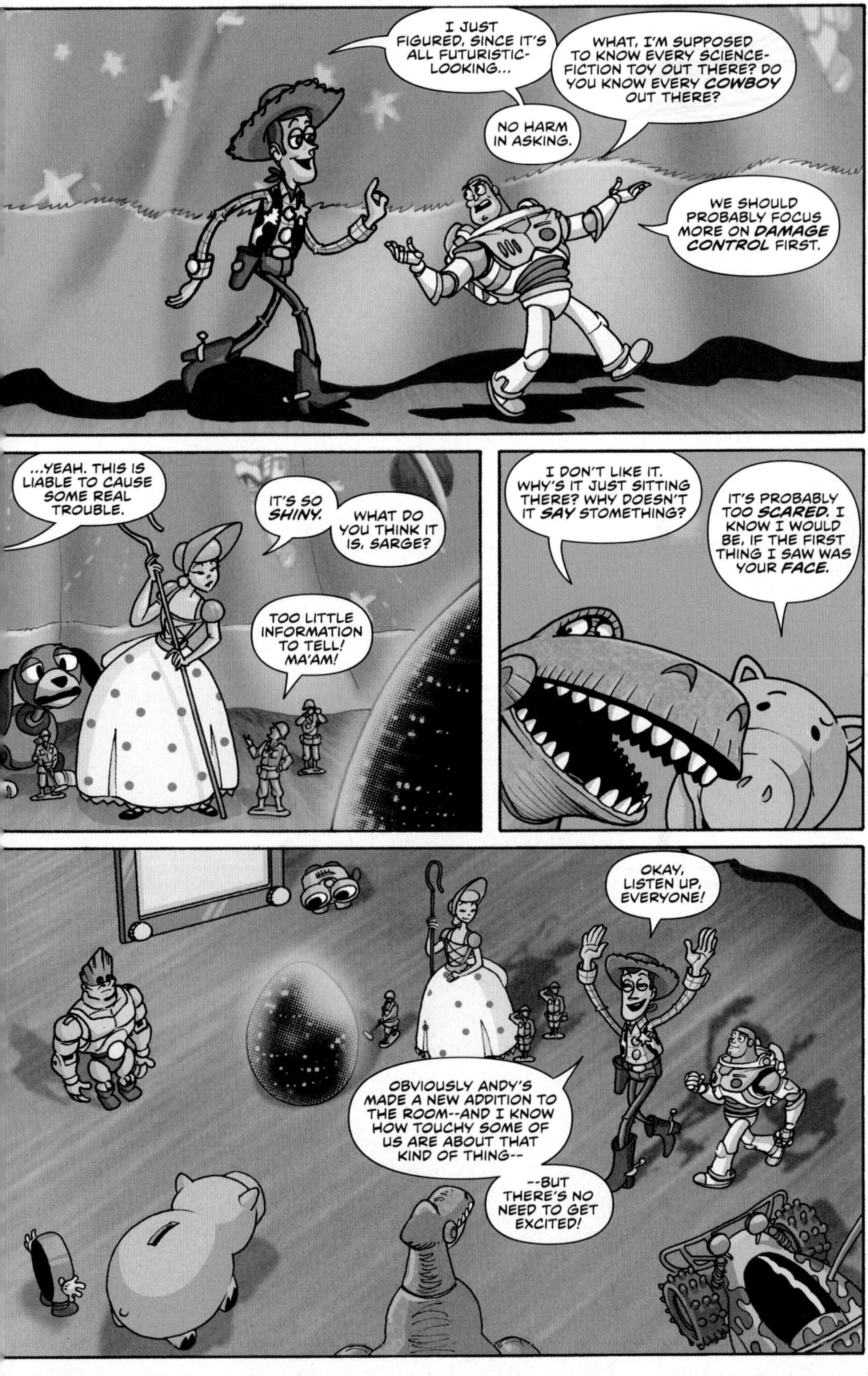

I JUST FIGURED, SINCE IT'S ALL FUTURISTIC-LOOKING...
NO HARM IN ASKING.
WHAT, I'M SUPPOSED TO KNOW EVERY SCIENCE-FICTION TOY OUT THERE? DO YOU KNOW EVERY *COWBOY* OUT THERE?
WE SHOULD PROBABLY FOCUS MORE ON *DAMAGE CONTROL* FIRST.
...YEAH. THIS IS LIABLE TO CAUSE SOME REAL TROUBLE.
IT'S SO *SHINY.*
WHAT DO YOU THINK IT IS, SARGE?
TOO LITTLE INFORMATION TO TELL! MA'AM!
I DON'T LIKE IT. WHY'S IT JUST SITTING THERE? WHY DOESN'T IT *SAY* STOMETHING?
IT'S PROBABLY TOO *SCARED.* I KNOW I WOULD BE, IF THE FIRST THING I SAW WAS YOUR *FACE.*
OKAY, LISTEN UP, EVERYONE!
OBVIOUSLY ANDY'S MADE A NEW ADDITION TO THE ROOM--AND I KNOW HOW TOUCHY SOME OF US ARE ABOUT THAT KIND OF THING--
--BUT THERE'S NO NEED TO GET EXCITED!

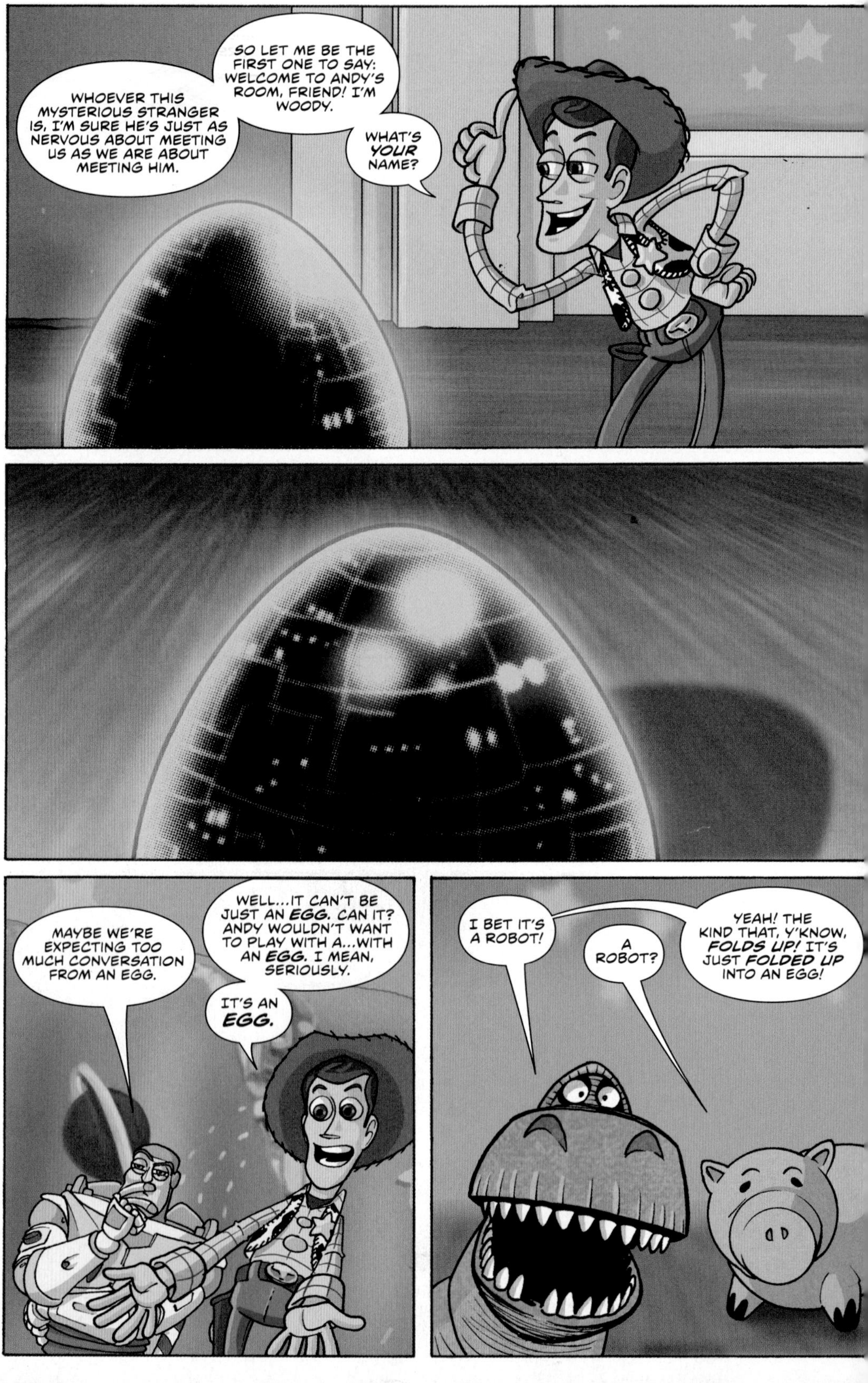
WHOEVER THIS MYSTERIOUS STRANGER IS, I'M SURE HE'S JUST AS NERVOUS ABOUT MEETING US AS WE ARE ABOUT MEETING HIM.
SO LET ME BE THE FIRST ONE TO SAY: WELCOME TO ANDY'S ROOM, FRIEND! I'M WOODY.
WHAT'S *YOUR* NAME?
MAYBE WE'RE EXPECTING TOO MUCH CONVERSATION FROM AN EGG.
WELL...IT CAN'T BE JUST AN *EGG.* CAN IT? ANDY WOULDN'T WANT TO PLAY WITH A...WITH AN *EGG.* I MEAN, SERIOUSLY.
IT'S AN *EGG.*
I BET IT'S A ROBOT!
A ROBOT?
YEAH! THE KIND THAT, Y'KNOW, *FOLDS UP!* IT'S JUST *FOLDED UP* INTO AN EGG!

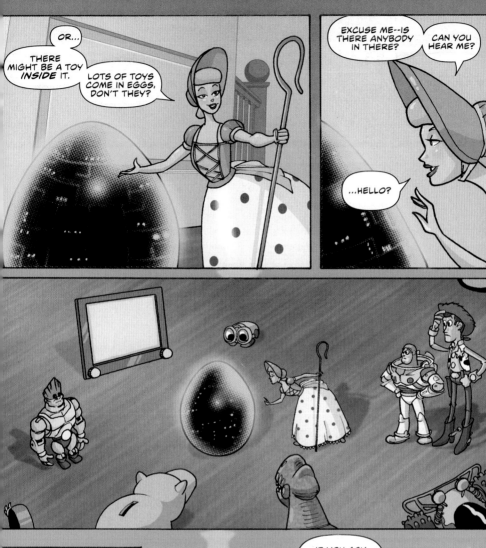

OR... THERE MIGHT BE A TOY *INSIDE* IT. LOTS OF TOYS COME IN EGGS, DON'T THEY?

EXCUSE ME--IS THERE ANYBODY IN THERE?

CAN YOU HEAR ME?

...HELLO?

HMPH.

IF YOU ASK ME, THAT'S ONE *UPPITY* EGG.

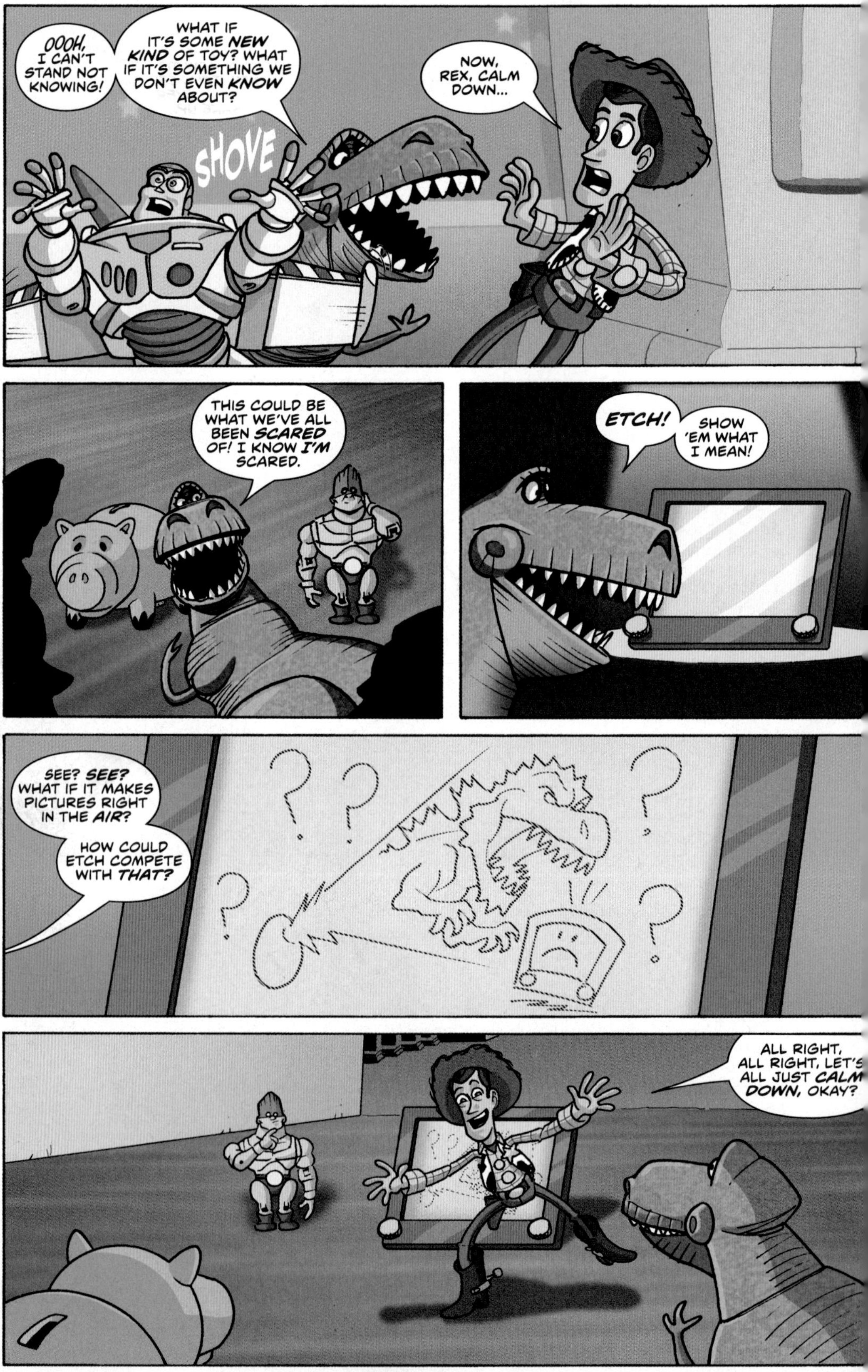
OOOH, I CAN'T STAND NOT KNOWING!
WHAT IF IT'S SOME NEW KIND OF TOY? WHAT IF IT'S SOMETHING WE DON'T EVEN KNOW ABOUT?
SHOVE
NOW, REX, CALM DOWN...
THIS COULD BE WHAT WE'VE ALL BEEN SCARED OF! I KNOW I'M SCARED.
ETCH!
SHOW 'EM WHAT I MEAN!
SEE? SEE? WHAT IF IT MAKES PICTURES RIGHT IN THE AIR?
HOW COULD ETCH COMPETE WITH THAT?
ALL RIGHT, ALL RIGHT, LET'S ALL JUST CALM DOWN, OKAY?

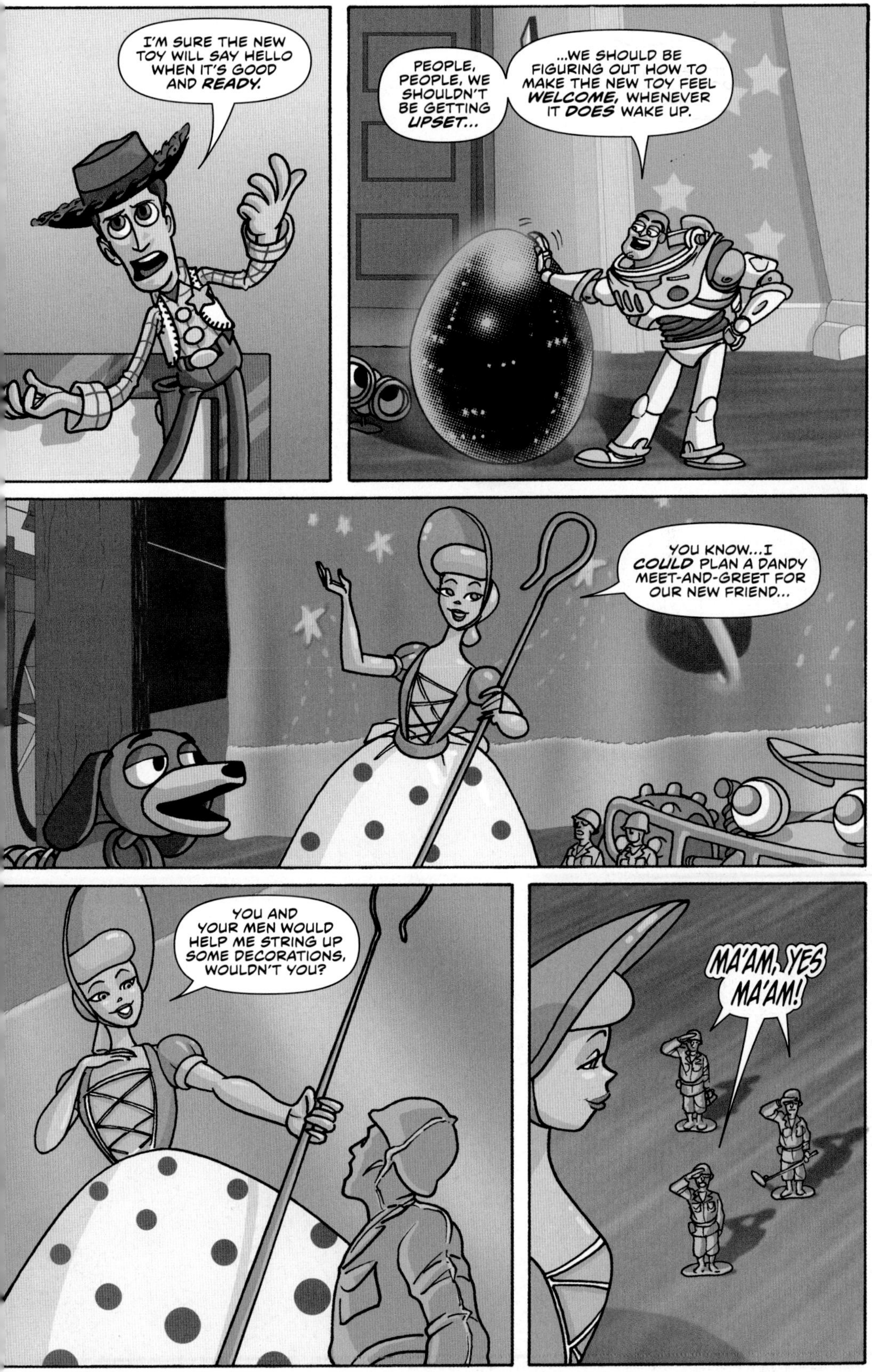
I'M SURE THE NEW TOY WILL SAY HELLO WHEN IT'S GOOD AND *READY.*
PEOPLE, PEOPLE, WE SHOULDN'T BE GETTING *UPSET...*
...WE SHOULD BE FIGURING OUT HOW TO MAKE THE NEW TOY FEEL *WELCOME,* WHENEVER IT *DOES* WAKE UP.
YOU KNOW...I *COULD* PLAN A DANDY MEET-AND-GREET FOR OUR NEW FRIEND...
YOU AND YOUR MEN WOULD HELP ME STRING UP SOME DECORATIONS, WOULDN'T YOU?
MA'AM, YES MA'AM!

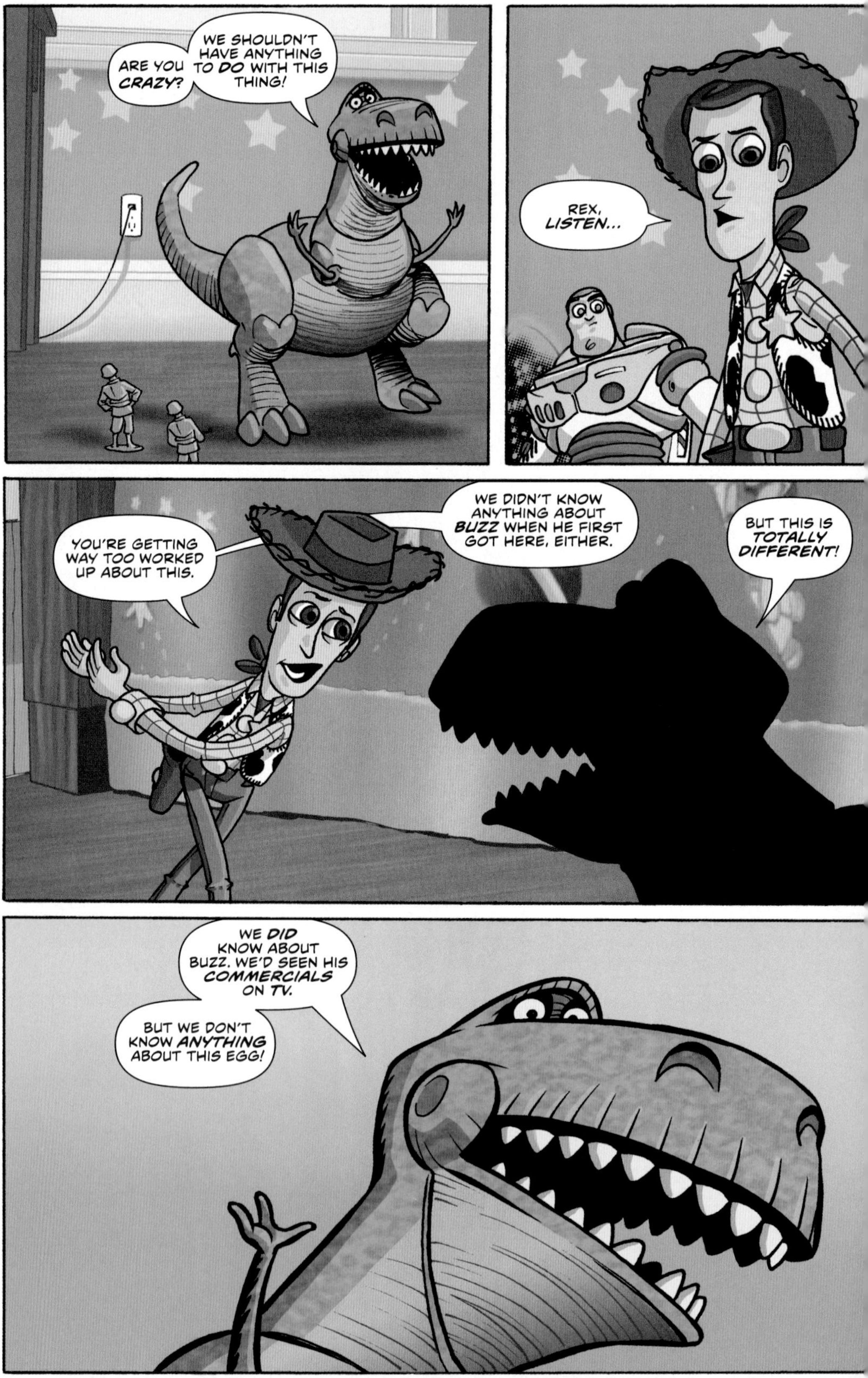
ARE YOU CRAZY?
WE SHOULDN'T HAVE ANYTHING TO DO WITH THIS THING!
REX, LISTEN...
YOU'RE GETTING WAY TOO WORKED UP ABOUT THIS.
WE DIDN'T KNOW ANYTHING ABOUT BUZZ WHEN HE FIRST GOT HERE, EITHER.
BUT THIS IS TOTALLY DIFFERENT!
WE DID KNOW ABOUT BUZZ. WE'D SEEN HIS COMMERCIALS ON TV.
BUT WE DON'T KNOW ANYTHING ABOUT THIS EGG!

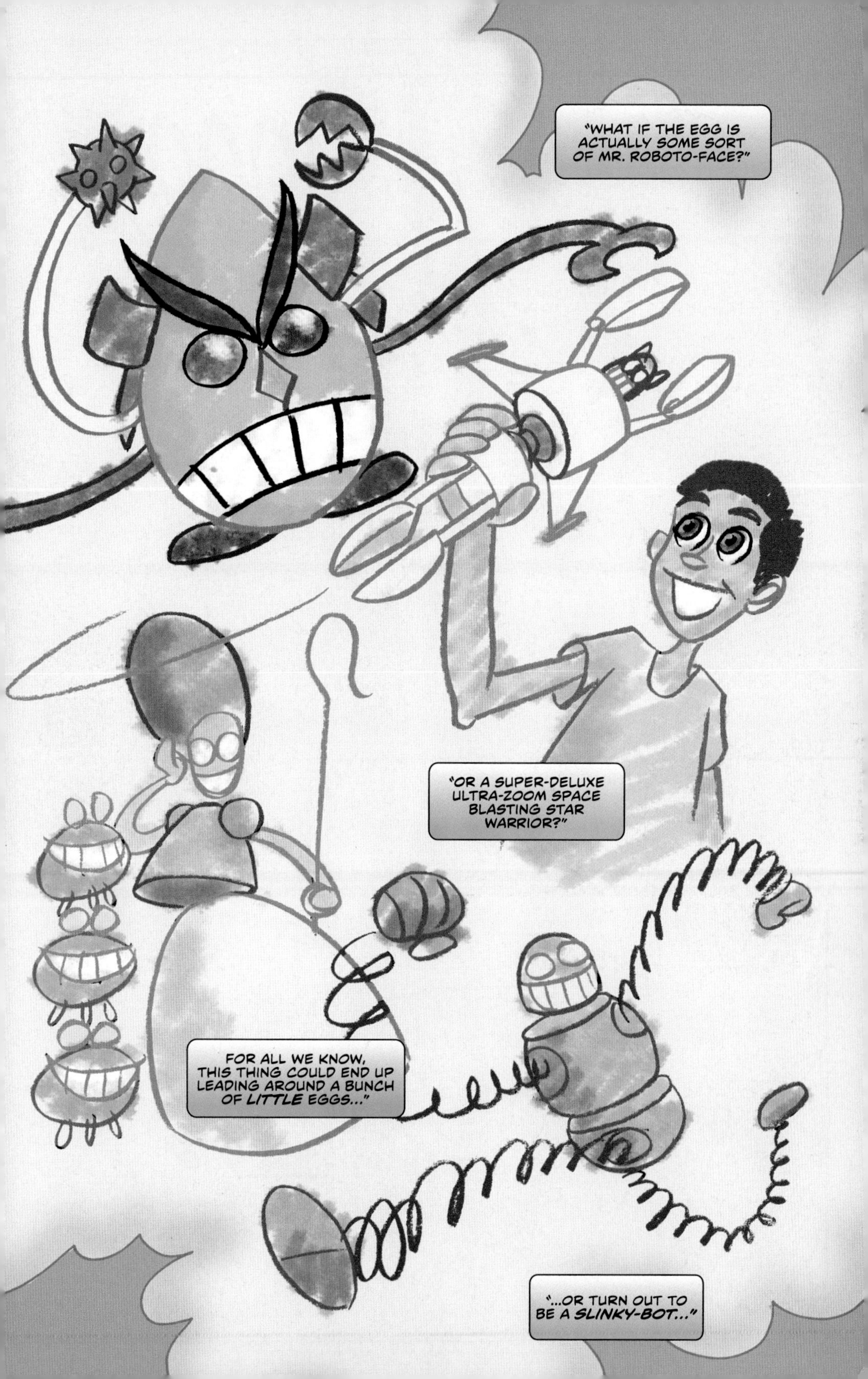
"WHAT IF THE EGG IS ACTUALLY SOME SORT OF MR. ROBOTO-FACE?"
"OR A SUPER-DELUXE ULTRA-ZOOM SPACE BLASTING STAR WARRIOR?"
FOR ALL WE KNOW, THIS THING COULD END UP LEADING AROUND A BUNCH OF *LITTLE* EGGS..."
"...OR TURN OUT TO BE A *SLINKY-BOT*..."

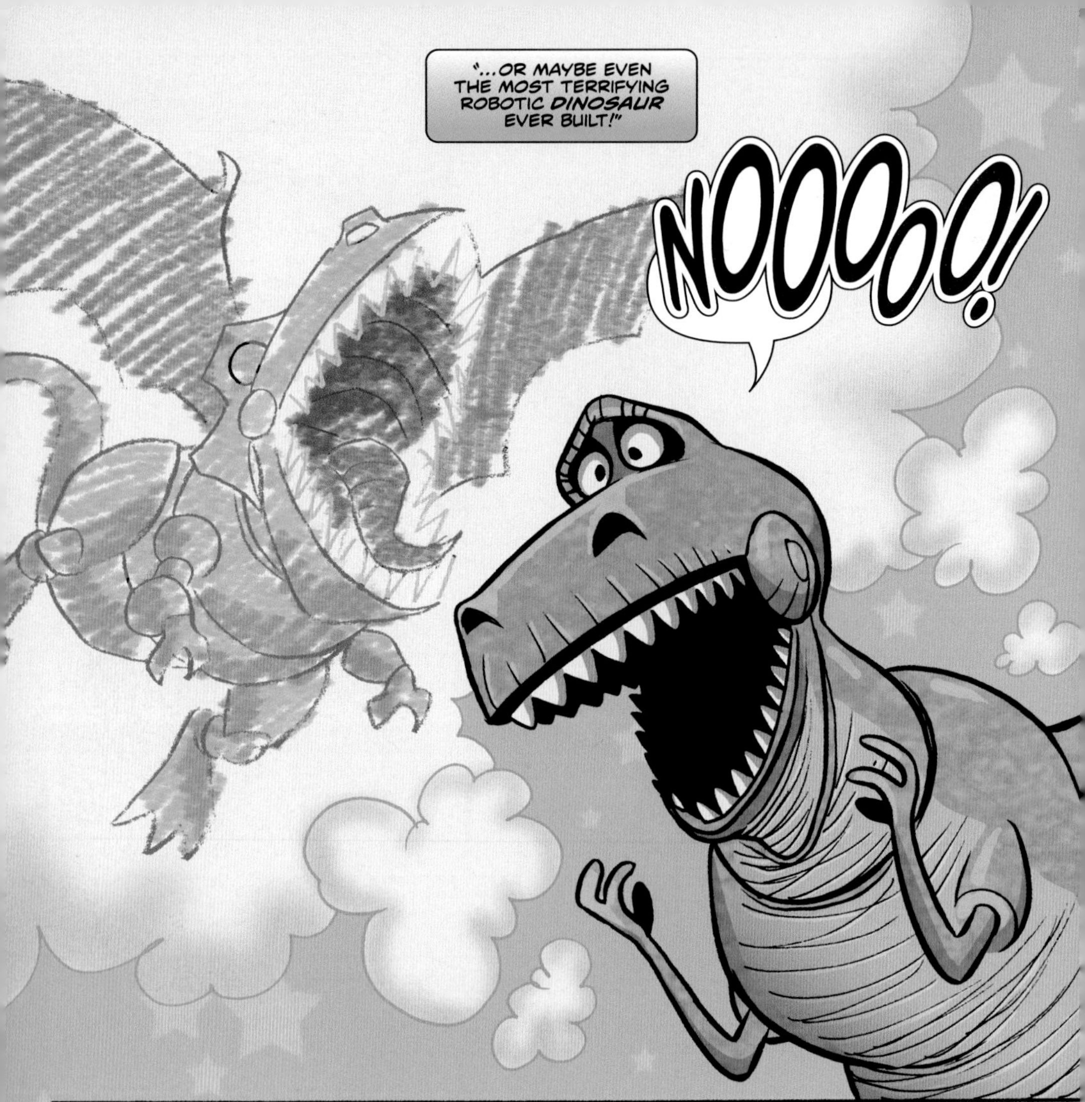
"...OR MAYBE EVEN THE MOST TERRIFYING ROBOTIC *DINOSAUR* EVER BUILT!"
NOOOOO!

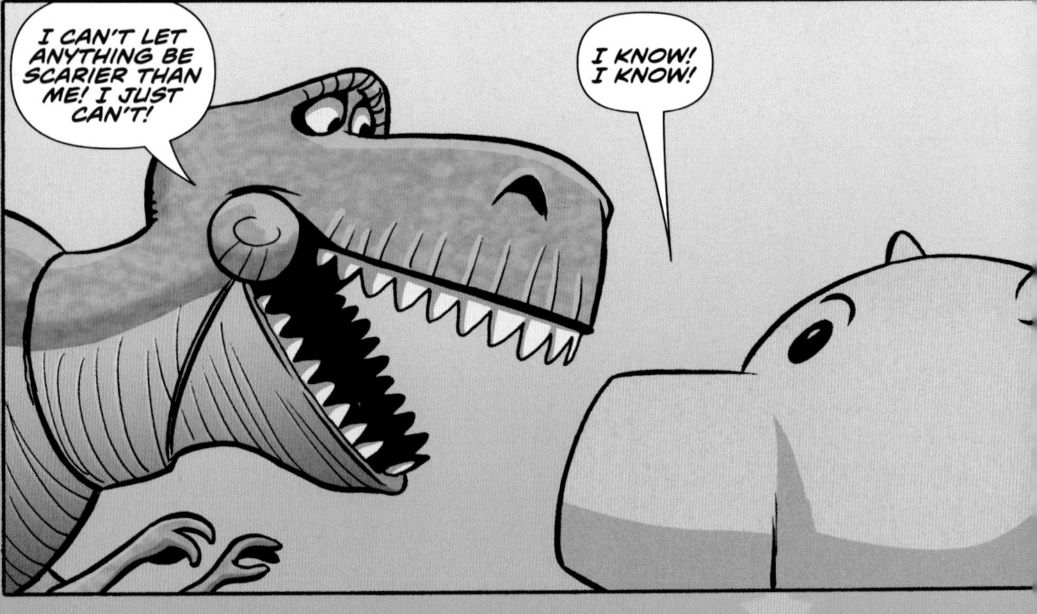
I CAN'T LET ANYTHING BE SCARIER THAN ME! I JUST CAN'T!
I KNOW! I KNOW!

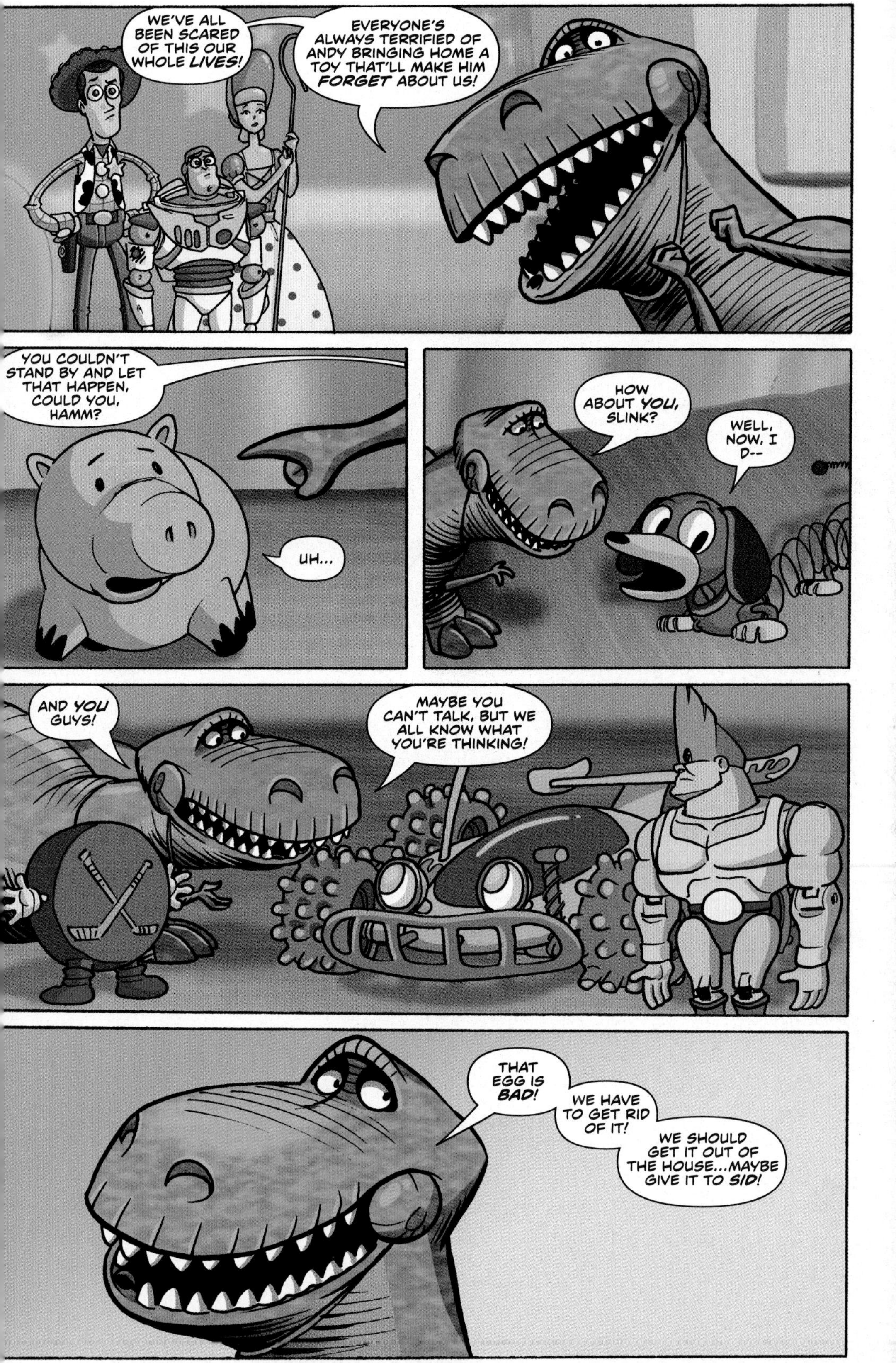
WE'VE ALL BEEN SCARED OF THIS OUR WHOLE *LIVES!*
EVERYONE'S ALWAYS TERRIFIED OF ANDY BRINGING HOME A TOY THAT'LL MAKE HIM *FORGET* ABOUT US!
YOU COULDN'T STAND BY AND LET THAT HAPPEN, COULD YOU, HAMM?
UH...
HOW ABOUT *YOU,* SLINK?
WELL, NOW, I D--
AND *YOU* GUYS!
MAYBE YOU CAN'T TALK, BUT WE ALL KNOW WHAT YOU'RE THINKING!
THAT EGG IS *BAD!*
WE HAVE TO GET RID OF IT!
WE SHOULD GET IT OUT OF THE HOUSE...MAYBE GIVE IT TO *SID!*

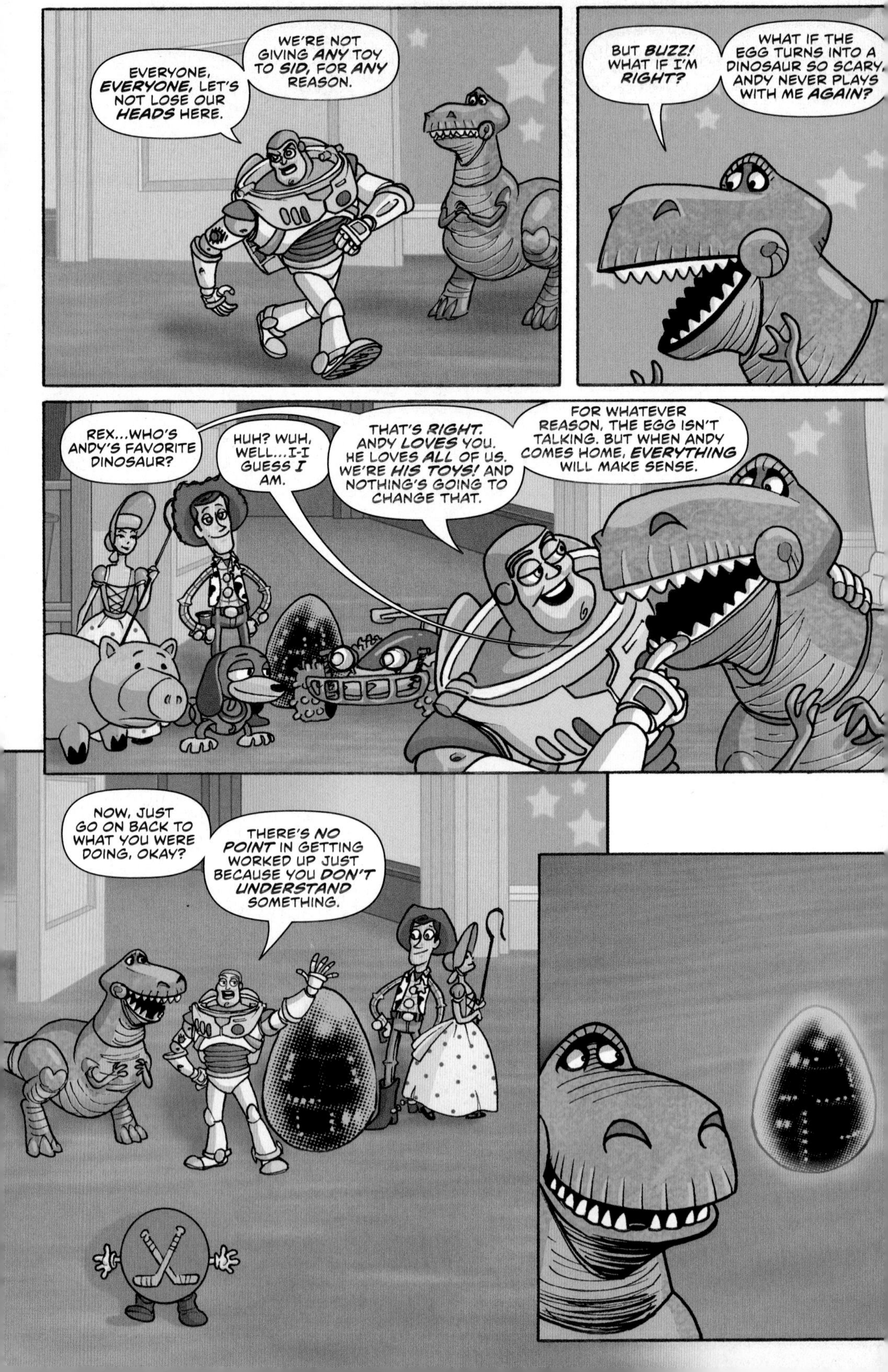
EVERYONE, EVERYONE, LET'S NOT LOSE OUR HEADS HERE.
WE'RE NOT GIVING ANY TOY TO SID, FOR ANY REASON.
BUT BUZZ! WHAT IF I'M RIGHT?
WHAT IF THE EGG TURNS INTO A DINOSAUR SO SCARY, ANDY NEVER PLAYS WITH ME AGAIN?
REX...WHO'S ANDY'S FAVORITE DINOSAUR?
HUH? WUH, WELL...I-I GUESS I AM.
THAT'S RIGHT. ANDY LOVES YOU. HE LOVES ALL OF US. WE'RE HIS TOYS! AND NOTHING'S GOING TO CHANGE THAT.
FOR WHATEVER REASON, THE EGG ISN'T TALKING. BUT WHEN ANDY COMES HOME, EVERYTHING WILL MAKE SENSE.
NOW, JUST GO ON BACK TO WHAT YOU WERE DOING, OKAY?
THERE'S NO POINT IN GETTING WORKED UP JUST BECAUSE YOU DON'T UNDERSTAND SOMETHING.

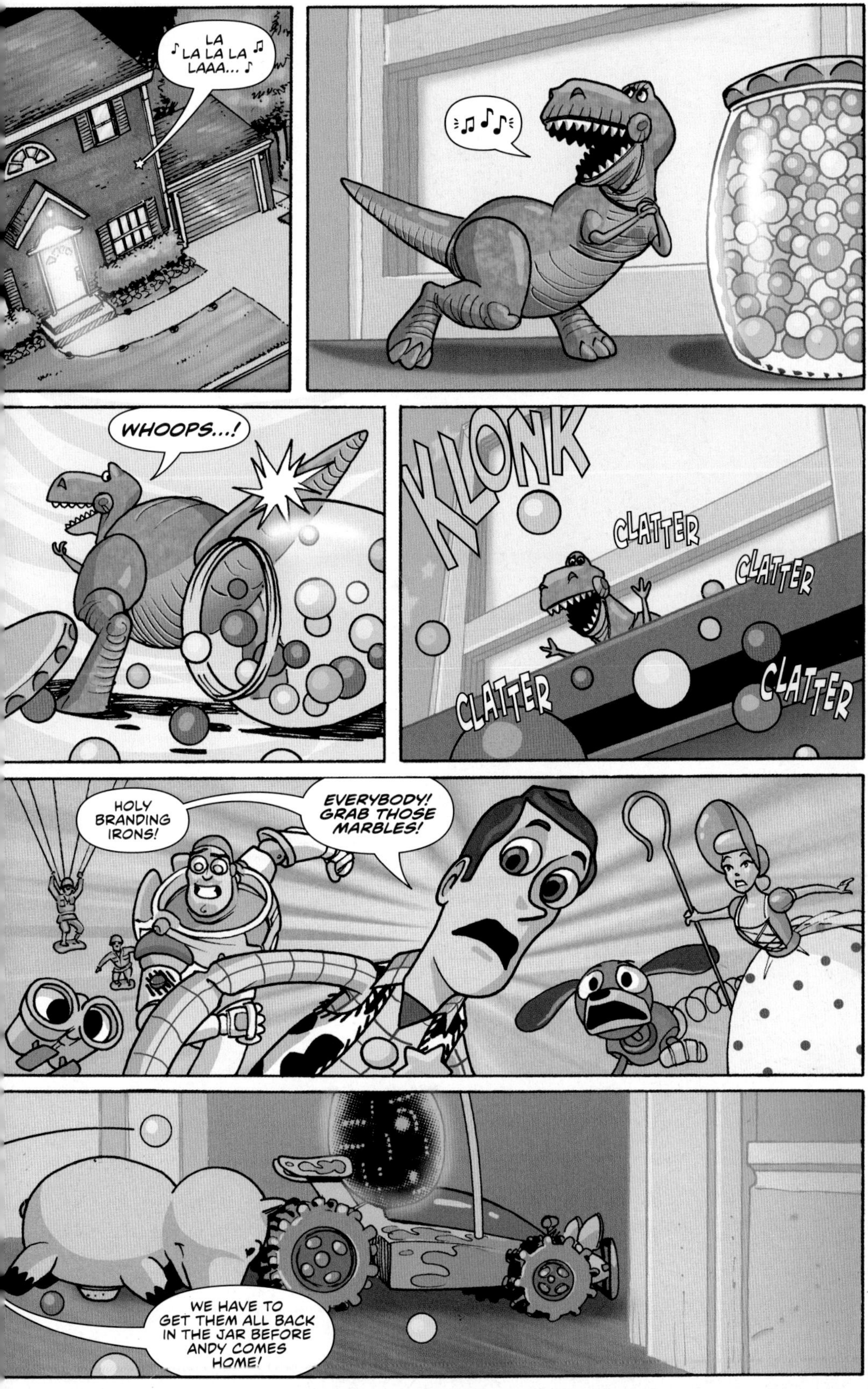

LA LA LA LA LAAA...
WHOOPS...!
KLONK
CLATTER
CLATTER
CLATTER
CLATTER
HOLY BRANDING IRONS!
EVERYBODY! GRAB THOSE MARBLES!
WE HAVE TO GET THEM ALL BACK IN THE JAR BEFORE ANDY COMES HOME!

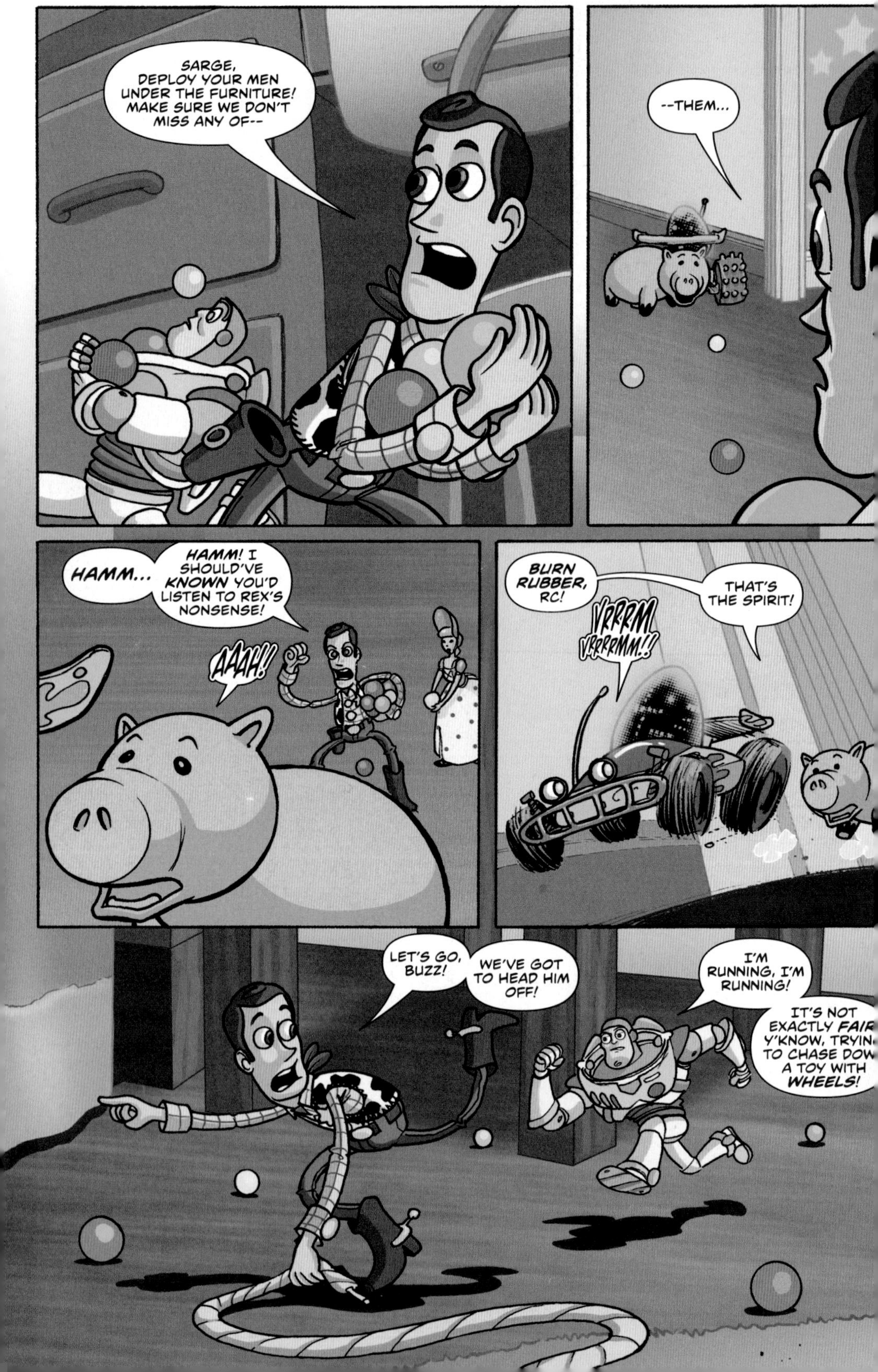
SARGE, DEPLOY YOUR MEN UNDER THE FURNITURE! MAKE SURE WE DON'T MISS ANY OF--
--THEM...
HAMM...
HAMM! I SHOULD'VE KNOWN YOU'D LISTEN TO REX'S NONSENSE!
AAAH!
BURN RUBBER, RC!
THAT'S THE SPIRIT!
VRRRM VRRRRMM!!
LET'S GO, BUZZ!
WE'VE GOT TO HEAD HIM OFF!
I'M RUNNING, I'M RUNNING!
IT'S NOT EXACTLY FAIR Y'KNOW, TRYIN TO CHASE DOW A TOY WITH WHEELS!

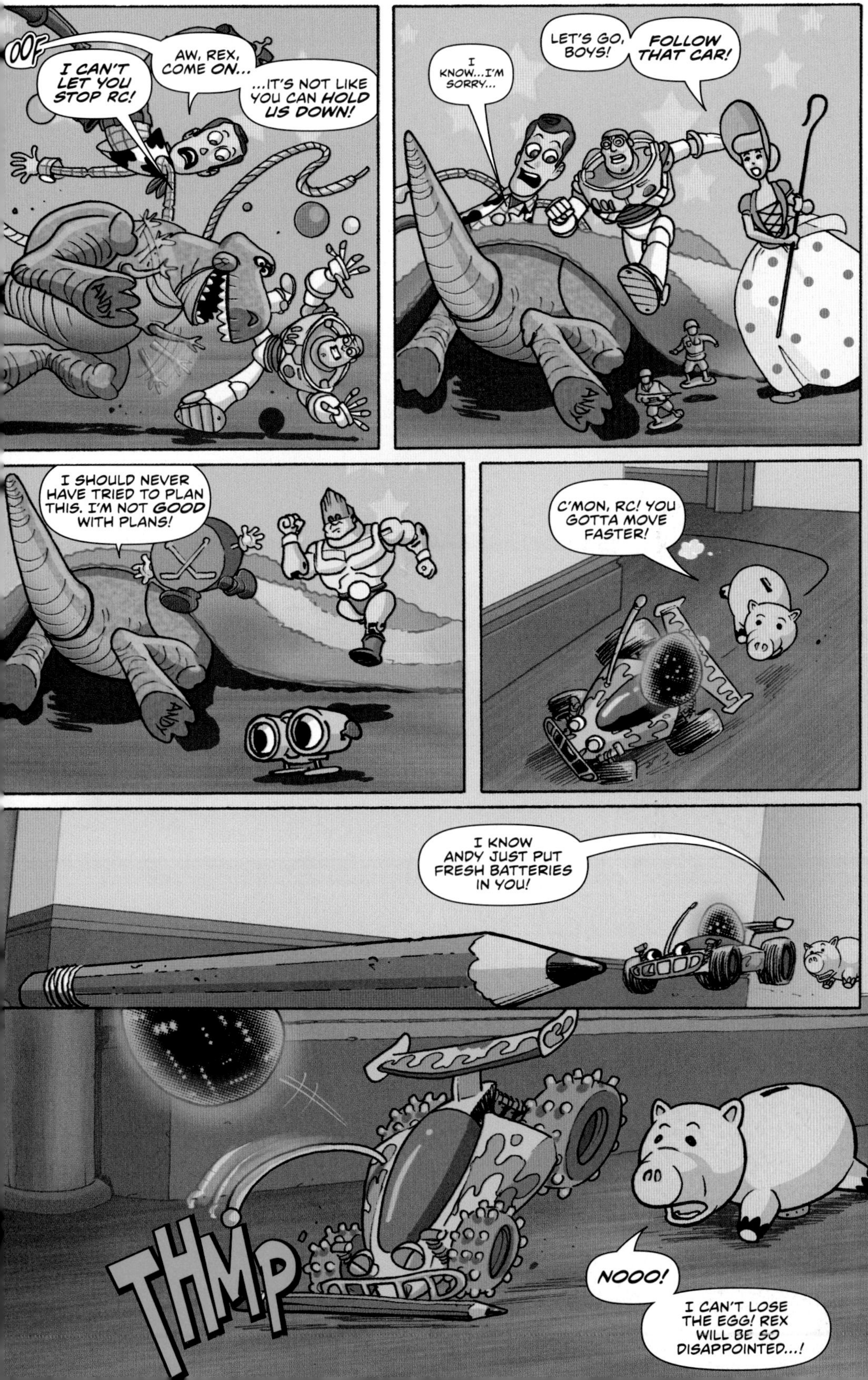

OOF
I CAN'T LET YOU STOP RC!
AW, REX, COME ON...
...IT'S NOT LIKE YOU CAN HOLD US DOWN!
I KNOW...I'M SORRY...
LET'S GO, BOYS!
FOLLOW THAT CAR!
I SHOULD NEVER HAVE TRIED TO PLAN THIS. I'M NOT GOOD WITH PLANS!
C'MON, RC! YOU GOTTA MOVE FASTER!
I KNOW ANDY JUST PUT FRESH BATTERIES IN YOU!
THMP
NOOO!
I CAN'T LOSE THE EGG! REX WILL BE SO DISAPPOINTED...!

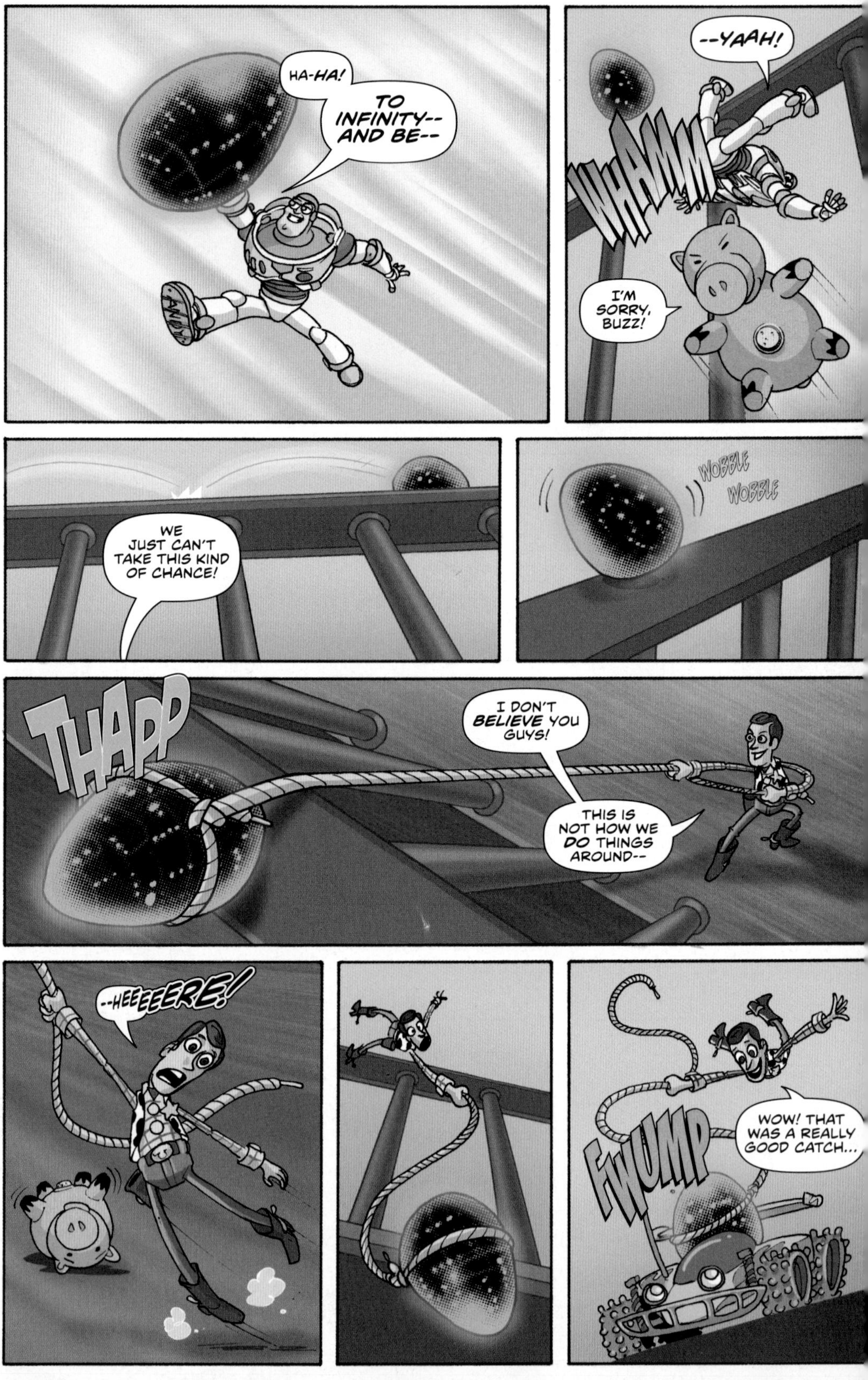

HA-HA!
TO INFINITY-- AND BE--
--YAAH!
WHAMM
I'M SORRY, BUZZ!
WE JUST CAN'T TAKE THIS KIND OF CHANCE!
WOBBLE
WOBBLE
THAPP
I DON'T BELIEVE YOU GUYS!
THIS IS NOT HOW WE DO THINGS AROUND--
--HEEEEERE!
FWUMP
WOW! THAT WAS A REALLY GOOD CATCH...

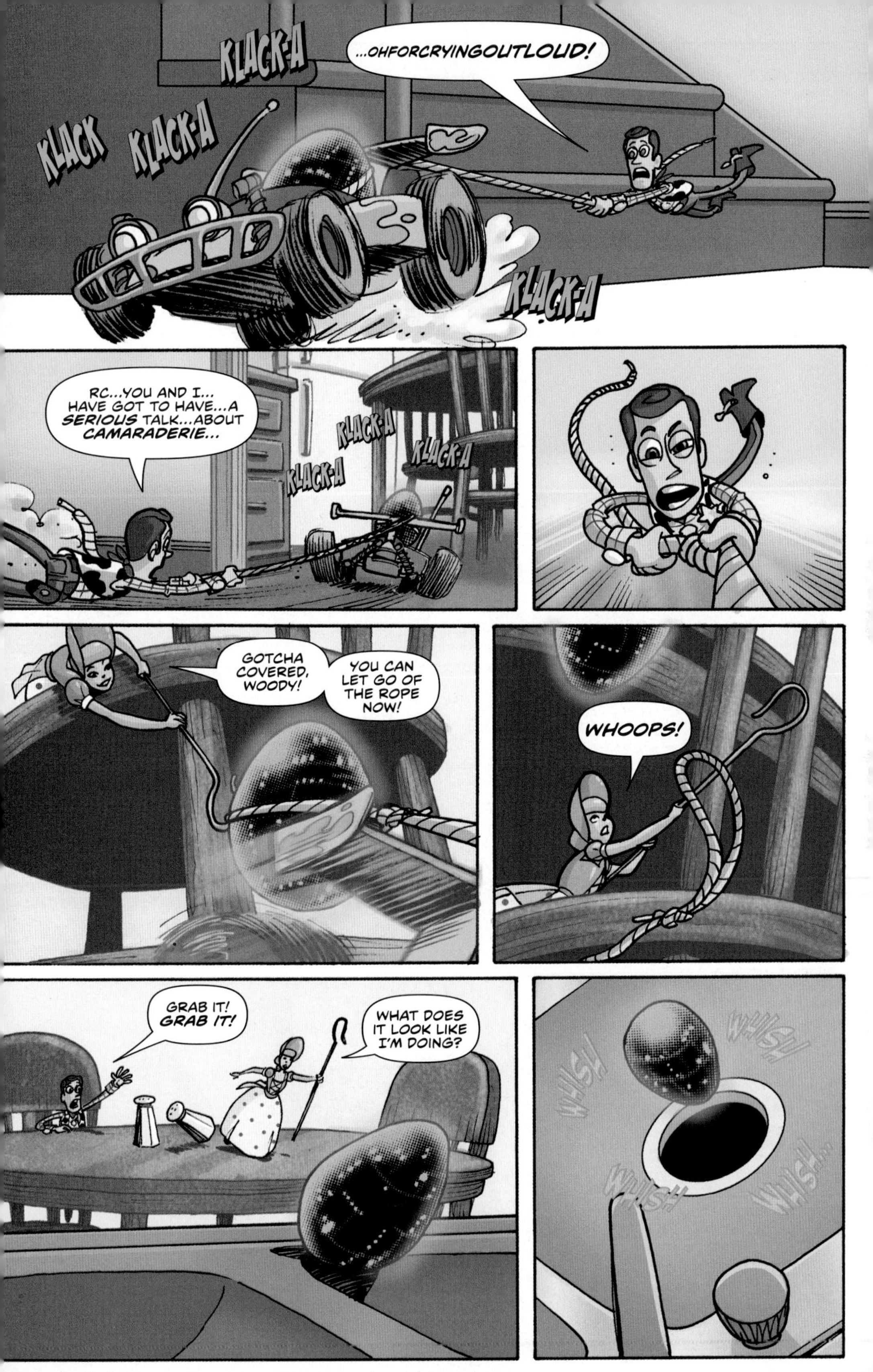
KLACK
KLACK-A
KLACK-A
...OHFORCRYINGOUTLOUD!
KLACK-A
RC...YOU AND I... HAVE GOT TO HAVE...A SERIOUS TALK...ABOUT CAMARADERIE...
KLACK-A
KLACK-A
KLACK-A
GOTCHA COVERED, WOODY!
YOU CAN LET GO OF THE ROPE NOW!
WHOOPS!
GRAB IT! GRAB IT!
WHAT DOES IT LOOK LIKE I'M DOING?
WHISH
WHISH
WHISH
WHISH...

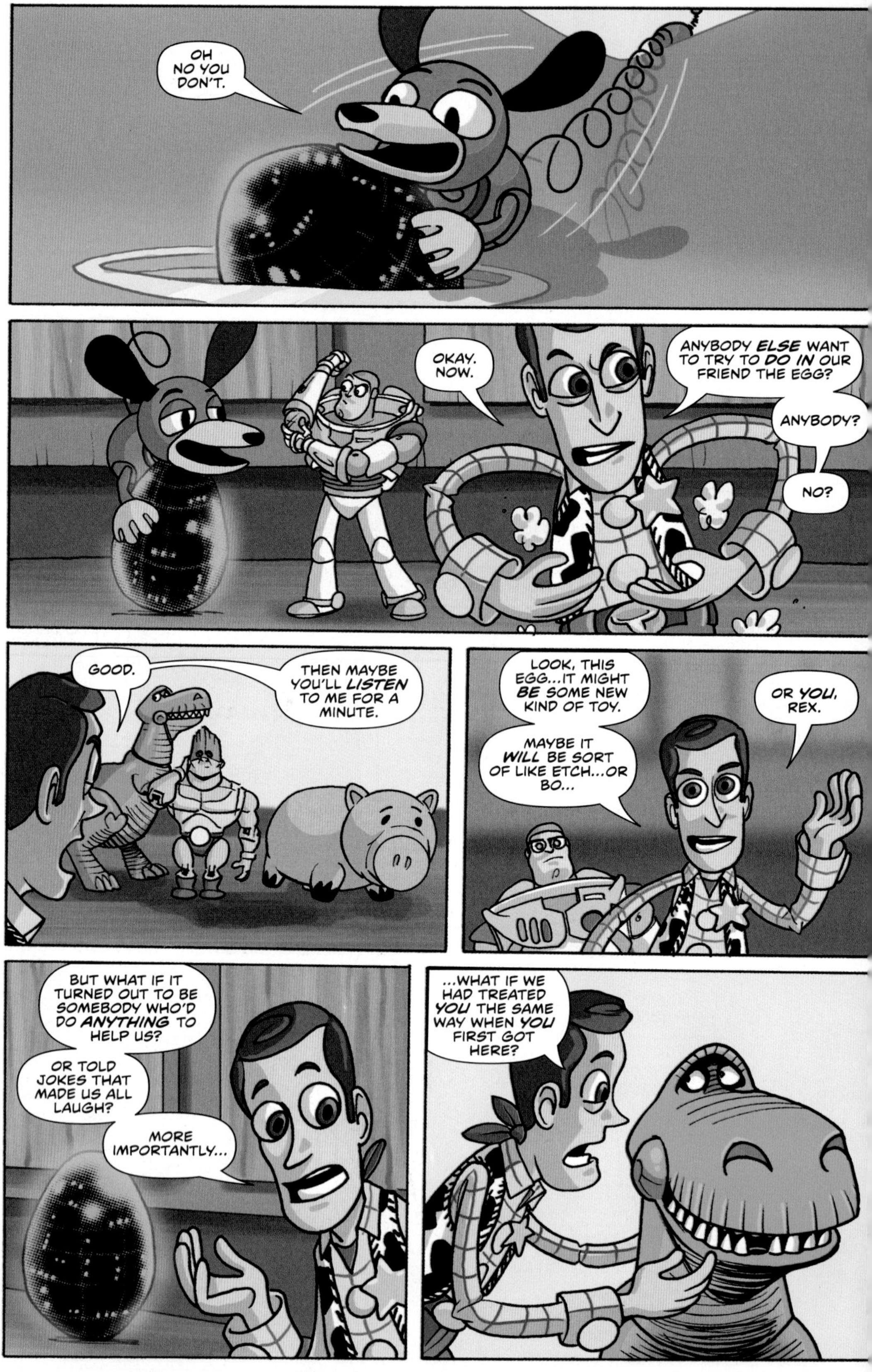
OH NO YOU DON'T.
OKAY. NOW.
ANYBODY ELSE WANT TO TRY TO DO IN OUR FRIEND THE EGG?
ANYBODY?
NO?
GOOD.
THEN MAYBE YOU'LL LISTEN TO ME FOR A MINUTE.
LOOK, THIS EGG...IT MIGHT BE SOME NEW KIND OF TOY.
MAYBE IT WILL BE SORT OF LIKE ETCH...OR BO...
OR YOU, REX.
BUT WHAT IF IT TURNED OUT TO BE SOMEBODY WHO'D DO ANYTHING TO HELP US?
OR TOLD JOKES THAT MADE US ALL LAUGH?
MORE IMPORTANTLY...
...WHAT IF WE HAD TREATED YOU THE SAME WAY WHEN YOU FIRST GOT HERE?

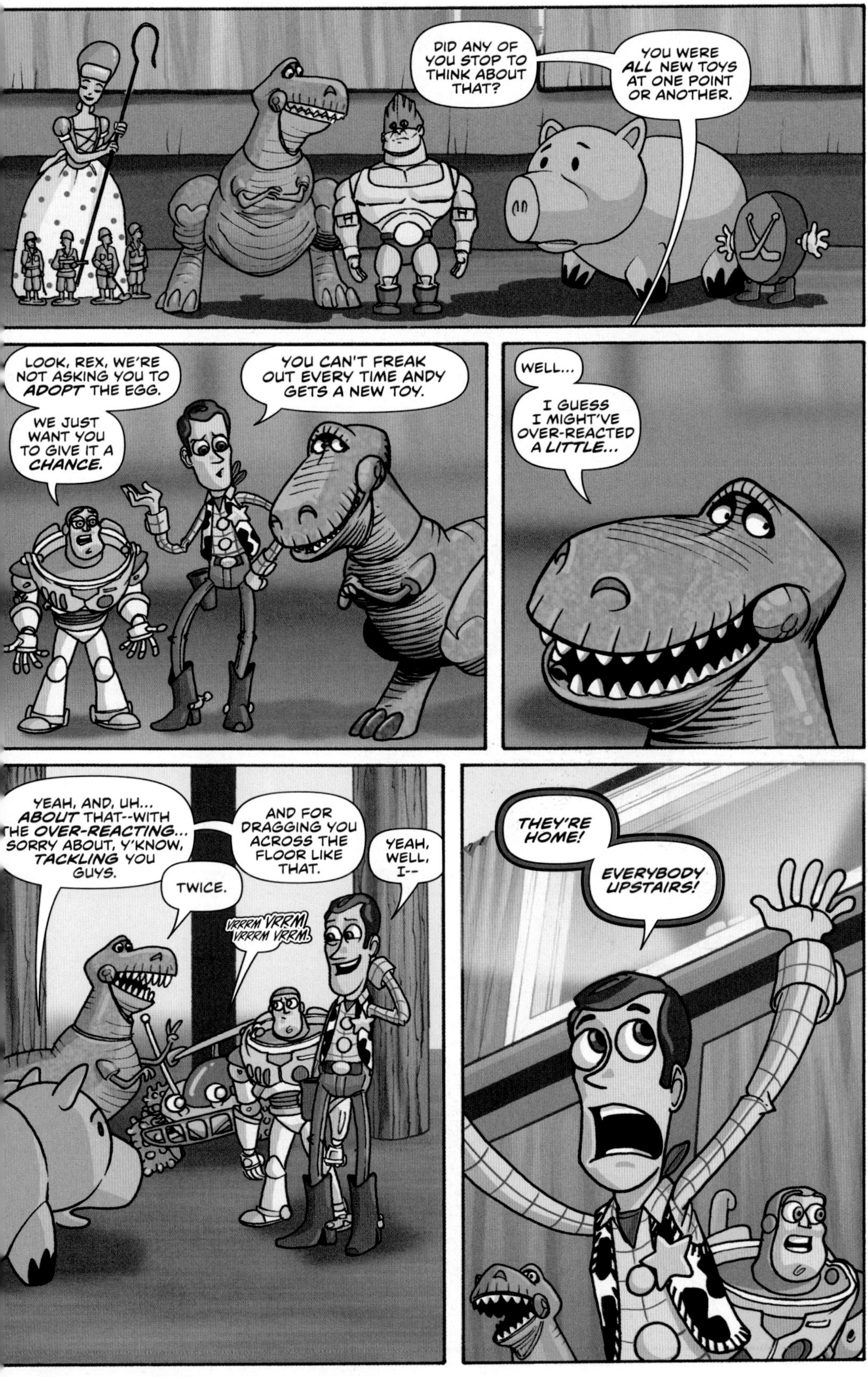
DID ANY OF YOU STOP TO THINK ABOUT THAT?
YOU WERE ALL NEW TOYS AT ONE POINT OR ANOTHER.
LOOK, REX, WE'RE NOT ASKING YOU TO ADOPT THE EGG.
WE JUST WANT YOU TO GIVE IT A CHANCE.
YOU CAN'T FREAK OUT EVERY TIME ANDY GETS A NEW TOY.
WELL...
I GUESS I MIGHT'VE OVER-REACTED A LITTLE...
YEAH, AND, UH... ABOUT THAT--WITH THE OVER-REACTING... SORRY ABOUT, Y'KNOW, TACKLING YOU GUYS.
TWICE.
AND FOR DRAGGING YOU ACROSS THE FLOOR LIKE THAT.
YEAH, WELL, I--
VRRRM VRRM VRRRM VRRM.
THEY'RE HOME!
EVERYBODY UPSTAIRS!

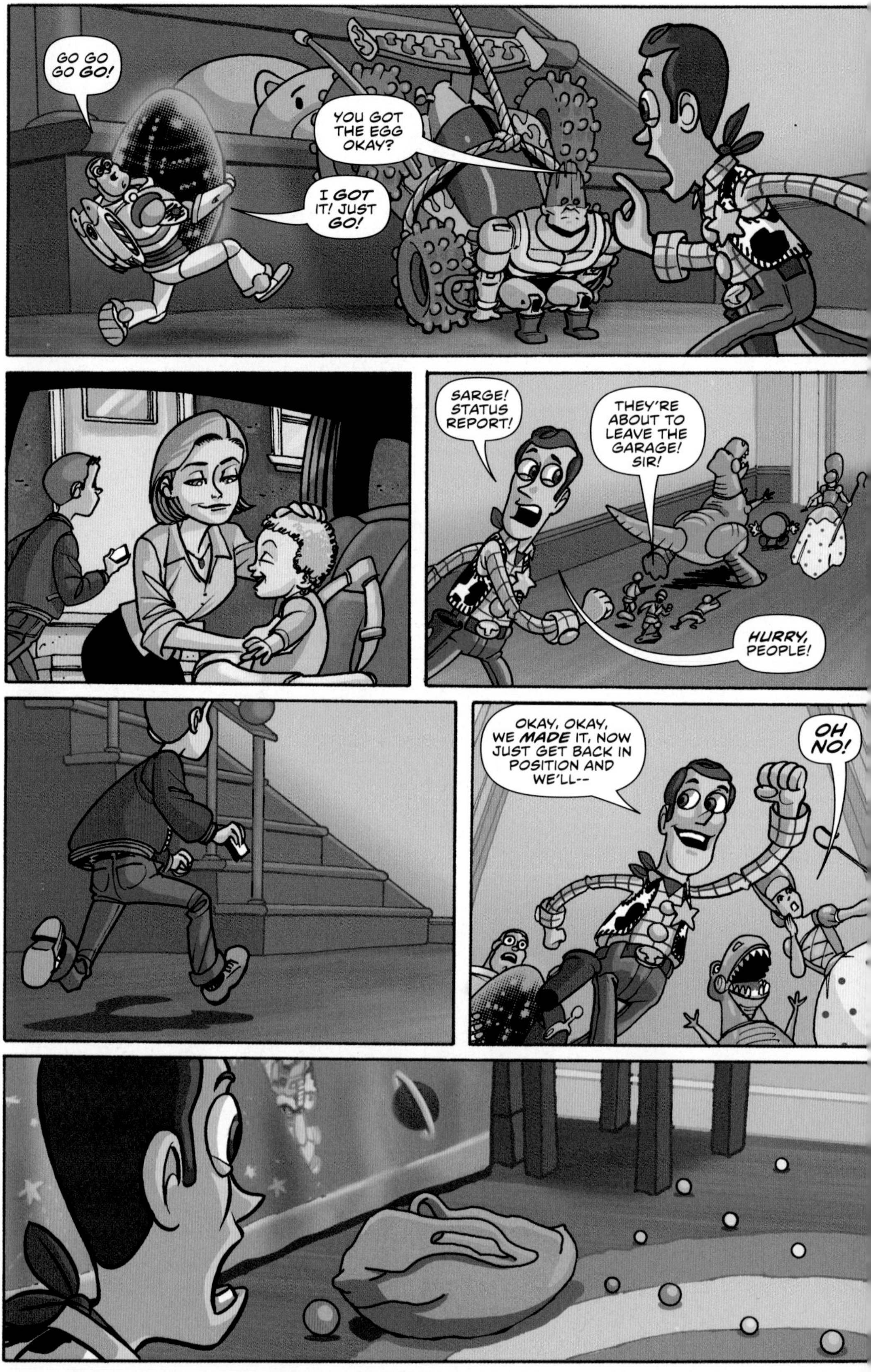
GO GO GO GO!
YOU GOT THE EGG OKAY?
I GOT IT! JUST GO!
SARGE! STATUS REPORT!
THEY'RE ABOUT TO LEAVE THE GARAGE! SIR!
HURRY, PEOPLE!
OKAY, OKAY, WE MADE IT, NOW JUST GET BACK IN POSITION AND WE'LL--
OH NO!

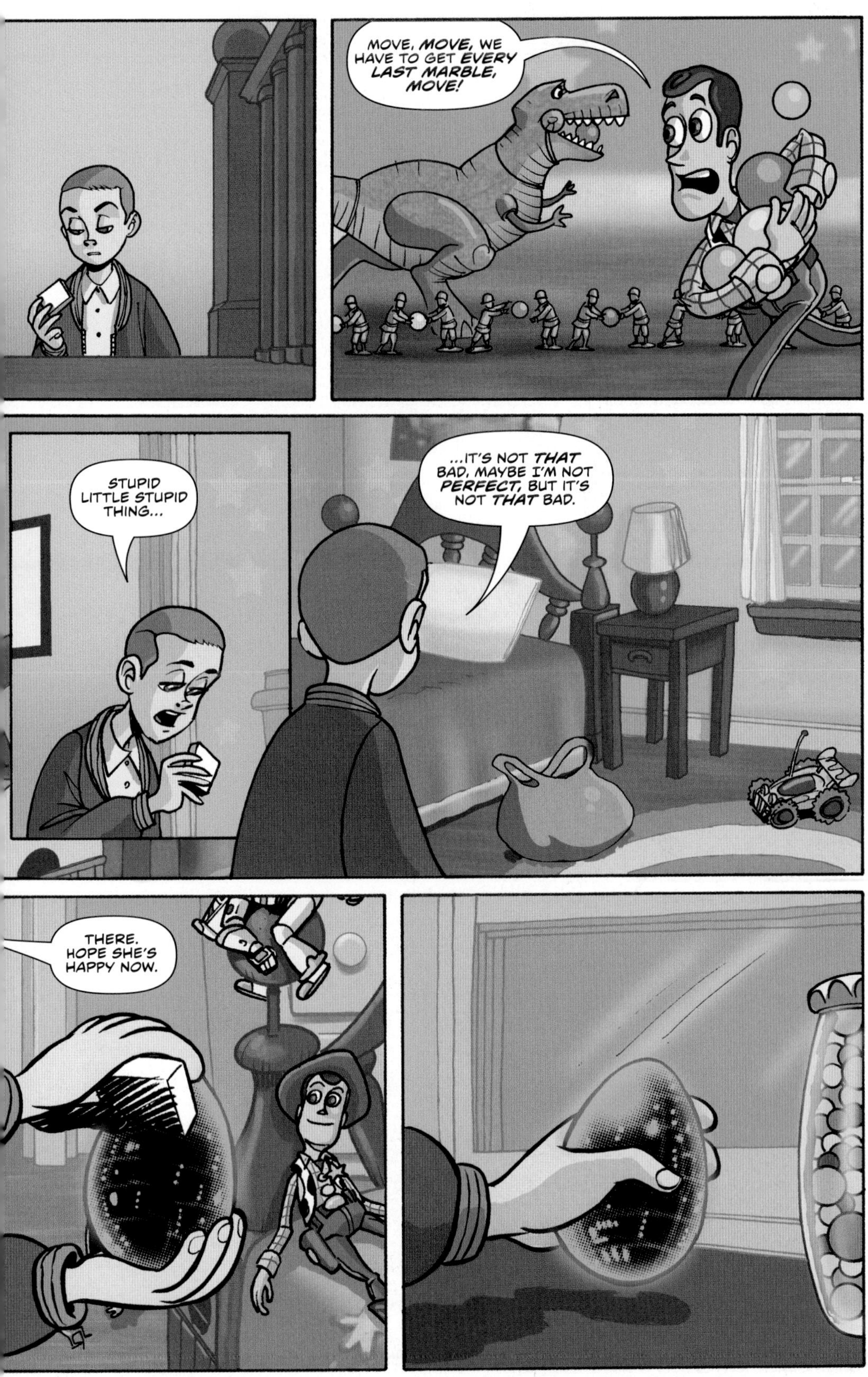
MOVE, MOVE, WE HAVE TO GET EVERY LAST MARBLE, MOVE!
STUPID LITTLE STUPID THING...
...IT'S NOT THAT BAD, MAYBE I'M NOT PERFECT, BUT IT'S NOT THAT BAD.
THERE. HOPE SHE'S HAPPY NOW.

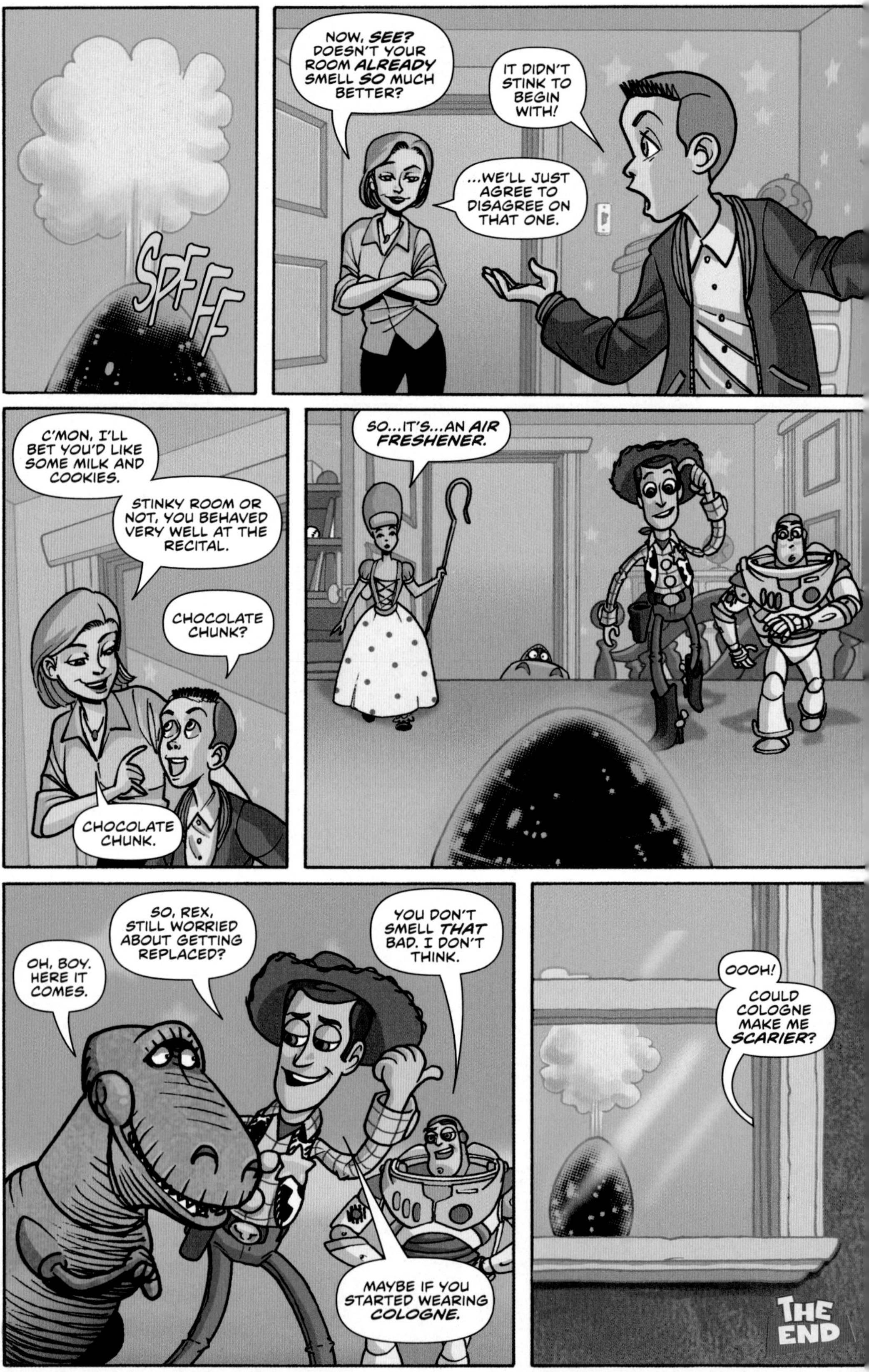
SPFFFF
NOW, SEE? DOESN'T YOUR ROOM ALREADY SMELL SO MUCH BETTER?
IT DIDN'T STINK TO BEGIN WITH!
...WE'LL JUST AGREE TO DISAGREE ON THAT ONE.
C'MON, I'LL BET YOU'D LIKE SOME MILK AND COOKIES.
STINKY ROOM OR NOT, YOU BEHAVED VERY WELL AT THE RECITAL.
CHOCOLATE CHUNK?
CHOCOLATE CHUNK.
SO...IT'S...AN AIR FRESHENER.
OH, BOY. HERE IT COMES.
SO, REX, STILL WORRIED ABOUT GETTING REPLACED?
YOU DON'T SMELL THAT BAD. I DON'T THINK.
MAYBE IF YOU STARTED WEARING COLOGNE.
OOOH!
COULD COLOGNE MAKE ME SCARIER?
THE END

CHAPTER TWO

WEIRD SCIENCE

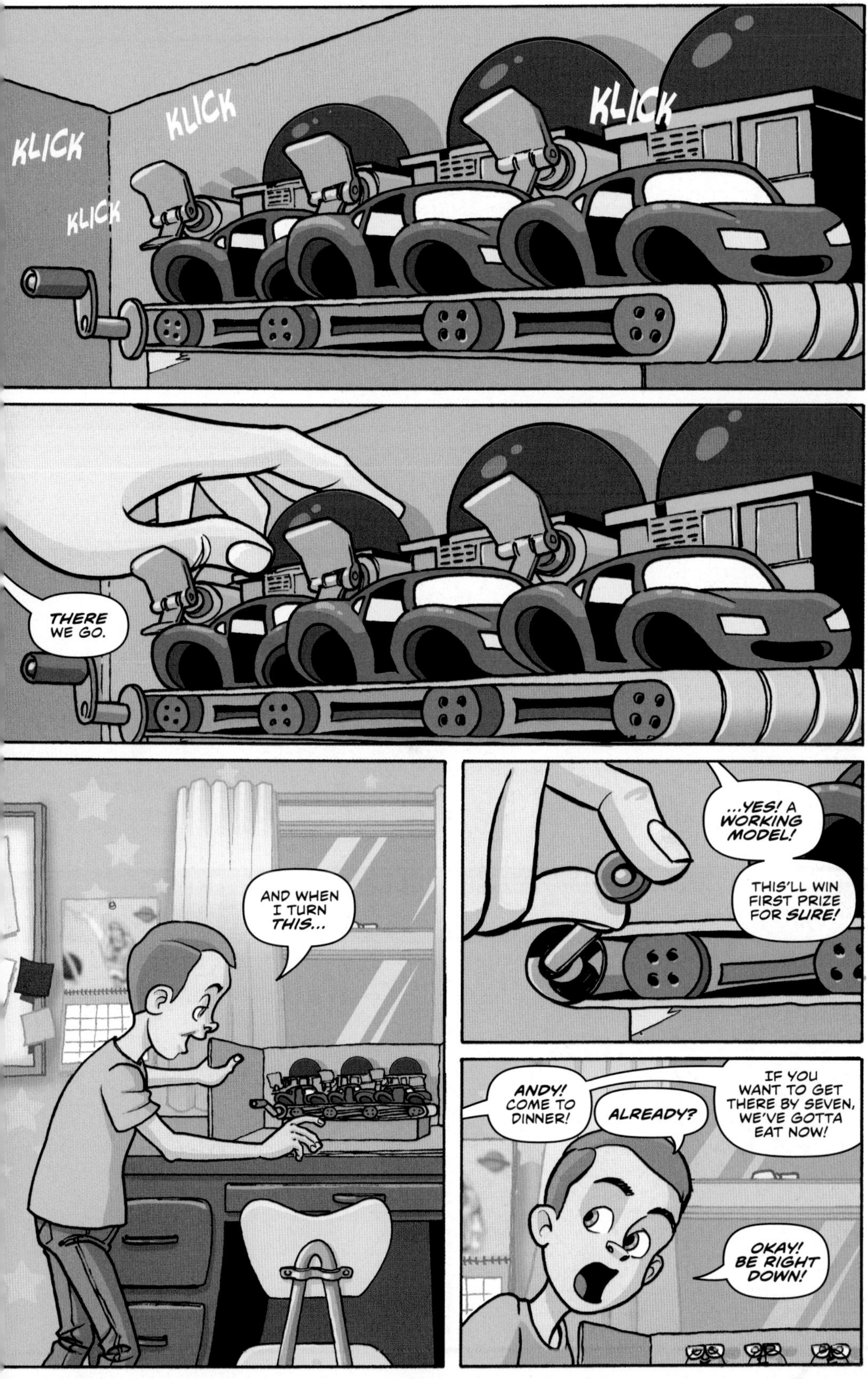
KLICK
KLICK
KLICK
KLICK
THERE WE GO.
AND WHEN I TURN THIS...
...YES! A WORKING MODEL!
THIS'LL WIN FIRST PRIZE FOR SURE!
ANDY! COME TO DINNER!
ALREADY?
IF YOU WANT TO GET THERE BY SEVEN, WE'VE GOTTA EAT NOW!
OKAY! BE RIGHT DOWN!

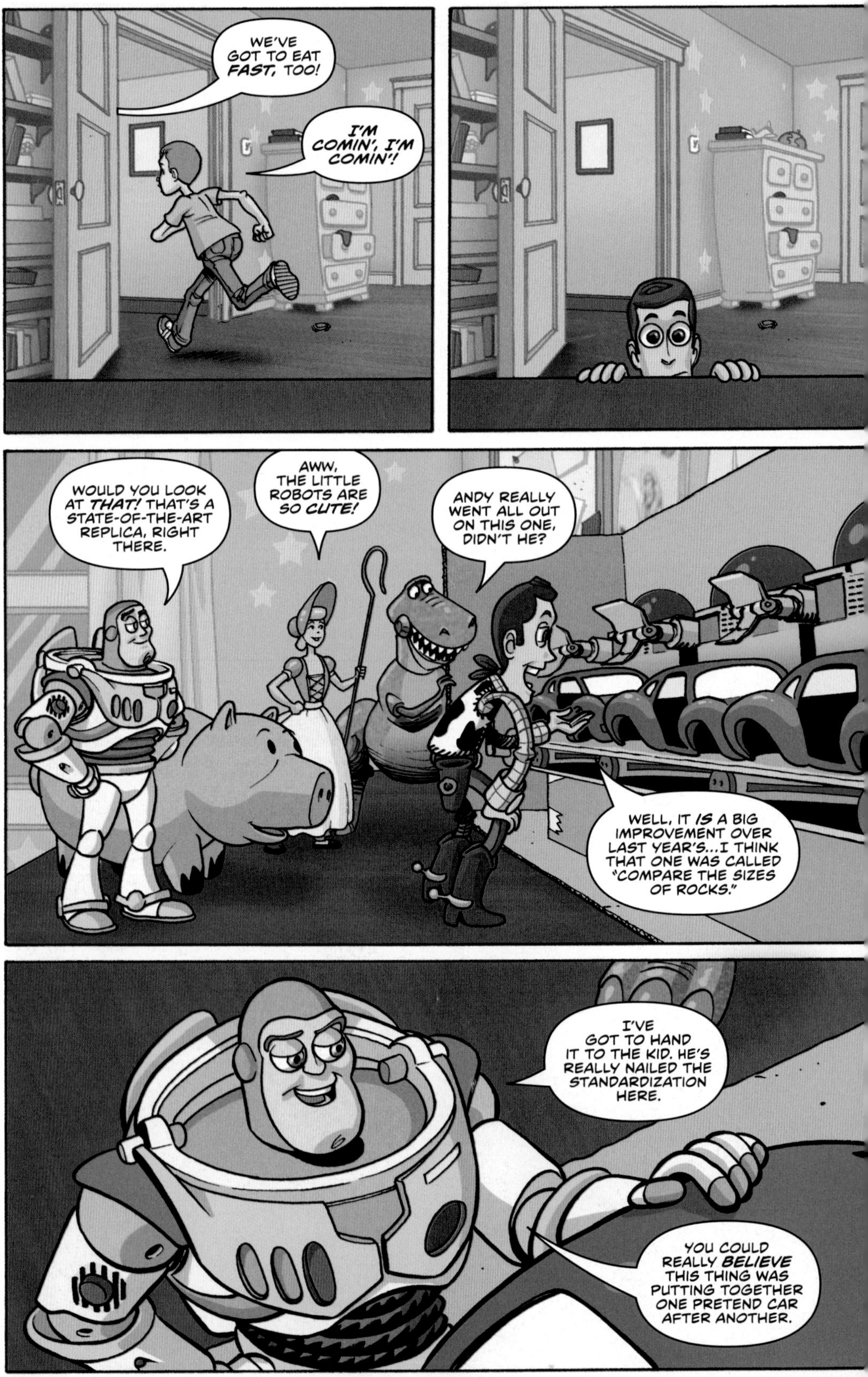
WE'VE GOT TO EAT *FAST,* TOO!
I'M COMIN', I'M COMIN'!
WOULD YOU LOOK AT *THAT!* THAT'S A STATE-OF-THE-ART REPLICA, RIGHT THERE.
AWW, THE LITTLE ROBOTS ARE SO *CUTE!*
ANDY REALLY WENT ALL OUT ON THIS ONE, DIDN'T HE?
WELL, IT *IS* A BIG IMPROVEMENT OVER LAST YEAR'S...I THINK THAT ONE WAS CALLED "COMPARE THE SIZES OF ROCKS."
I'VE GOT TO HAND IT TO THE KID. HE'S REALLY NAILED THE STANDARDIZATION HERE.
YOU COULD REALLY *BELIEVE* THIS THING WAS PUTTING TOGETHER ONE PRETEND CAR AFTER ANOTHER.

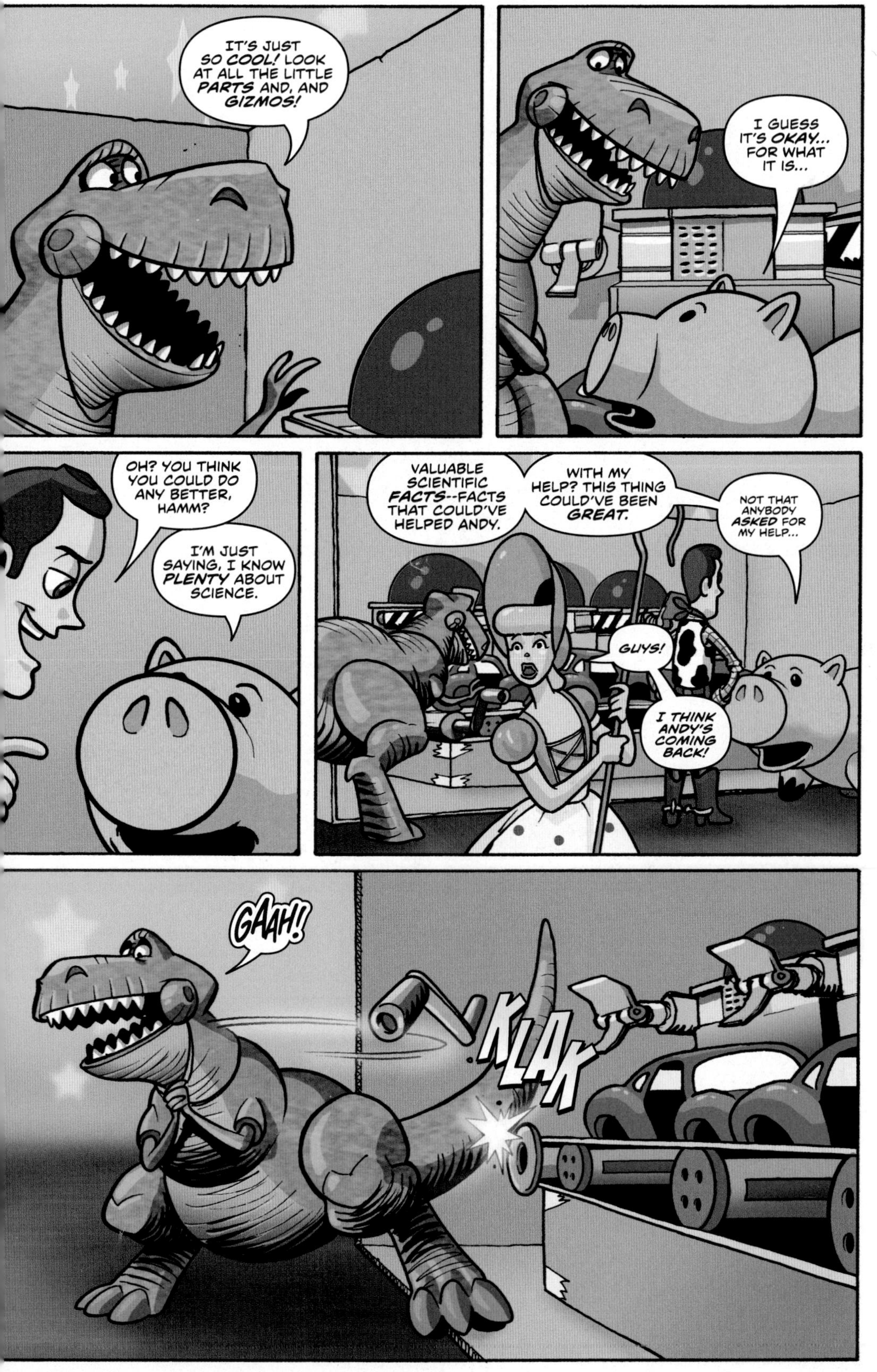
IT'S JUST SO *COOL!* LOOK AT ALL THE LITTLE *PARTS* AND, AND *GIZMOS!*
I GUESS IT'S *OKAY*... FOR WHAT IT IS...
OH? YOU THINK YOU COULD DO ANY BETTER, HAMM?
I'M JUST SAYING, I KNOW *PLENTY* ABOUT SCIENCE.
VALUABLE SCIENTIFIC *FACTS*--FACTS THAT COULD'VE HELPED ANDY.
WITH MY HELP? THIS THING COULD'VE BEEN *GREAT.*
NOT THAT ANYBODY *ASKED* FOR MY HELP...
GUYS!
I THINK ANDY'S COMING BACK!
GAAH!
KLAK

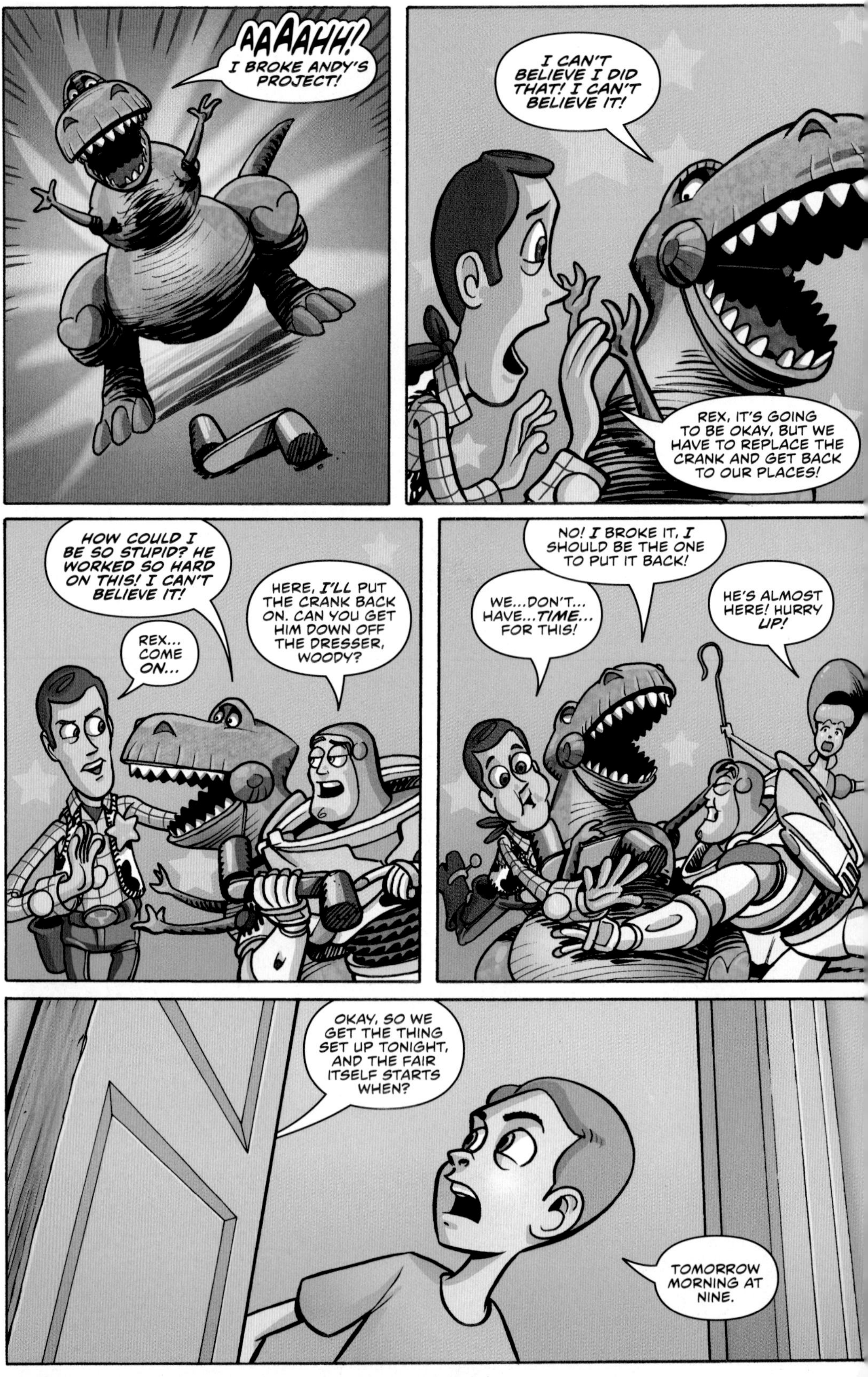
AAAAHH!
I BROKE ANDY'S PROJECT!
I CAN'T BELIEVE I DID THAT! I CAN'T BELIEVE IT!
REX, IT'S GOING TO BE OKAY, BUT WE HAVE TO REPLACE THE CRANK AND GET BACK TO OUR PLACES!
HOW COULD I BE SO STUPID? HE WORKED SO HARD ON THIS! I CAN'T BELIEVE IT!
REX... COME ON...
HERE, I'LL PUT THE CRANK BACK ON. CAN YOU GET HIM DOWN OFF THE DRESSER, WOODY?
NO! I BROKE IT, I SHOULD BE THE ONE TO PUT IT BACK!
WE...DON'T... HAVE...TIME... FOR THIS!
HE'S ALMOST HERE! HURRY UP!
OKAY, SO WE GET THE THING SET UP TONIGHT, AND THE FAIR ITSELF STARTS WHEN?
TOMORROW MORNING AT NINE.

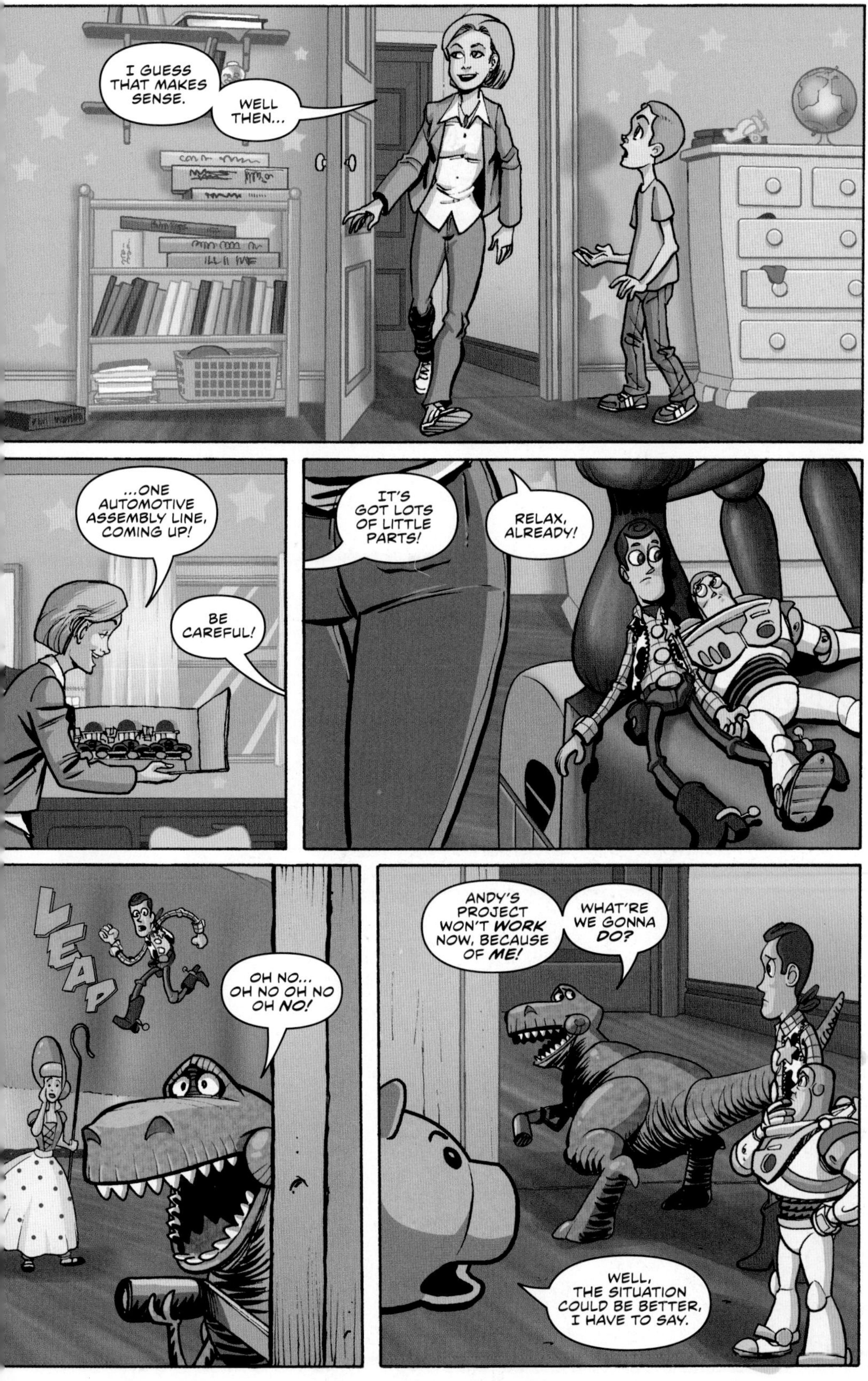
I GUESS THAT MAKES SENSE.
WELL THEN...
...ONE AUTOMOTIVE ASSEMBLY LINE, COMING UP!
BE CAREFUL!
IT'S GOT LOTS OF LITTLE PARTS!
RELAX, ALREADY!
LEAP
OH NO... OH NO OH NO OH *NO!*
ANDY'S PROJECT WON'T ***WORK*** NOW, BECAUSE OF ***ME!***
WHAT'RE WE GONNA ***DO?***
WELL, THE SITUATION COULD BE BETTER, I HAVE TO SAY.

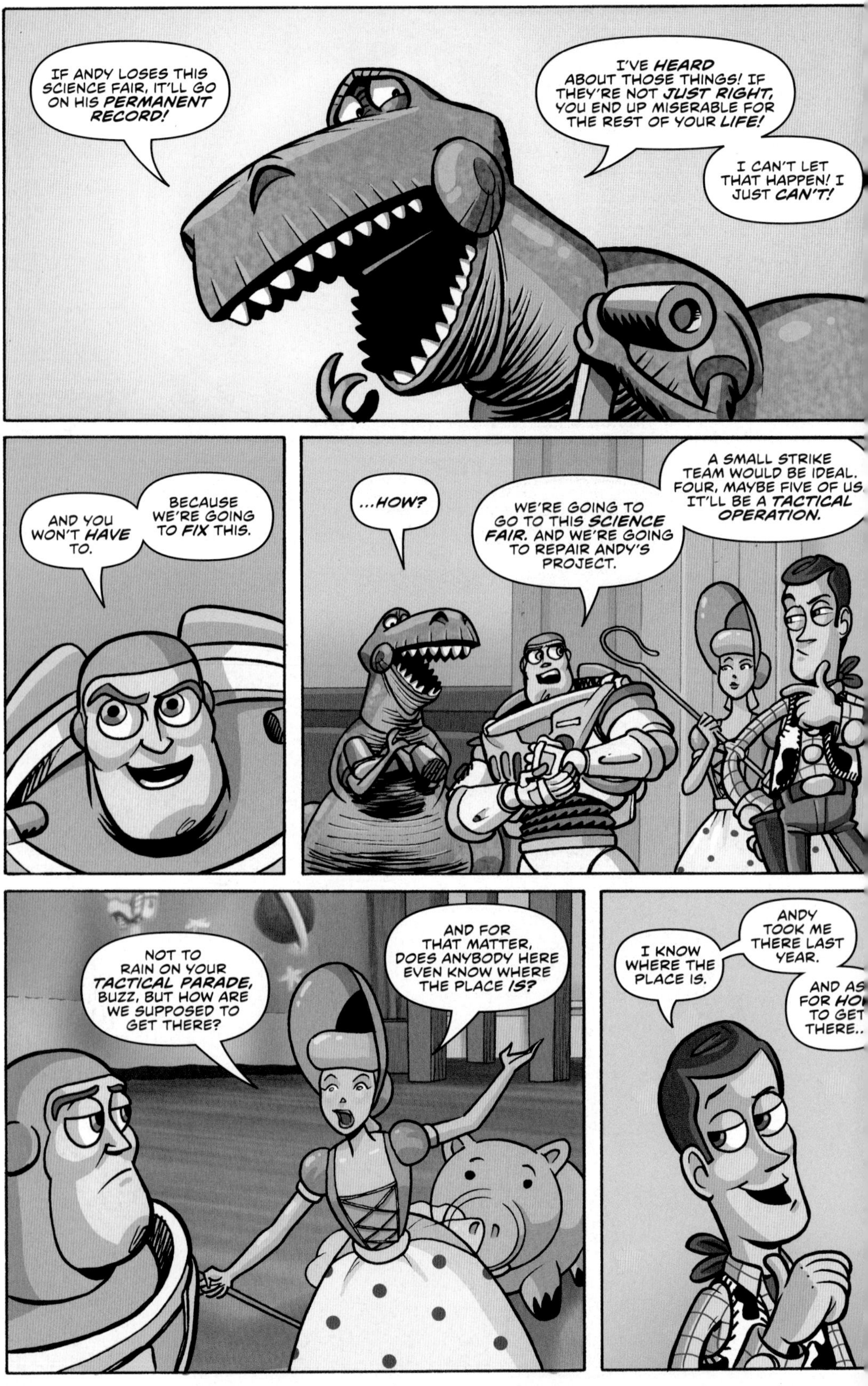
IF ANDY LOSES THIS SCIENCE FAIR, IT'LL GO ON HIS PERMANENT RECORD!
I'VE HEARD ABOUT THOSE THINGS! IF THEY'RE NOT JUST RIGHT, YOU END UP MISERABLE FOR THE REST OF YOUR LIFE!
I CAN'T LET THAT HAPPEN! I JUST CAN'T!
AND YOU WON'T HAVE TO.
BECAUSE WE'RE GOING TO FIX THIS.
...HOW?
WE'RE GOING TO GO TO THIS SCIENCE FAIR. AND WE'RE GOING TO REPAIR ANDY'S PROJECT.
A SMALL STRIKE TEAM WOULD BE IDEAL. FOUR, MAYBE FIVE OF US. IT'LL BE A TACTICAL OPERATION.
NOT TO RAIN ON YOUR TACTICAL PARADE, BUZZ, BUT HOW ARE WE SUPPOSED TO GET THERE?
AND FOR THAT MATTER, DOES ANYBODY HERE EVEN KNOW WHERE THE PLACE IS?
I KNOW WHERE THE PLACE IS.
ANDY TOOK ME THERE LAST YEAR.

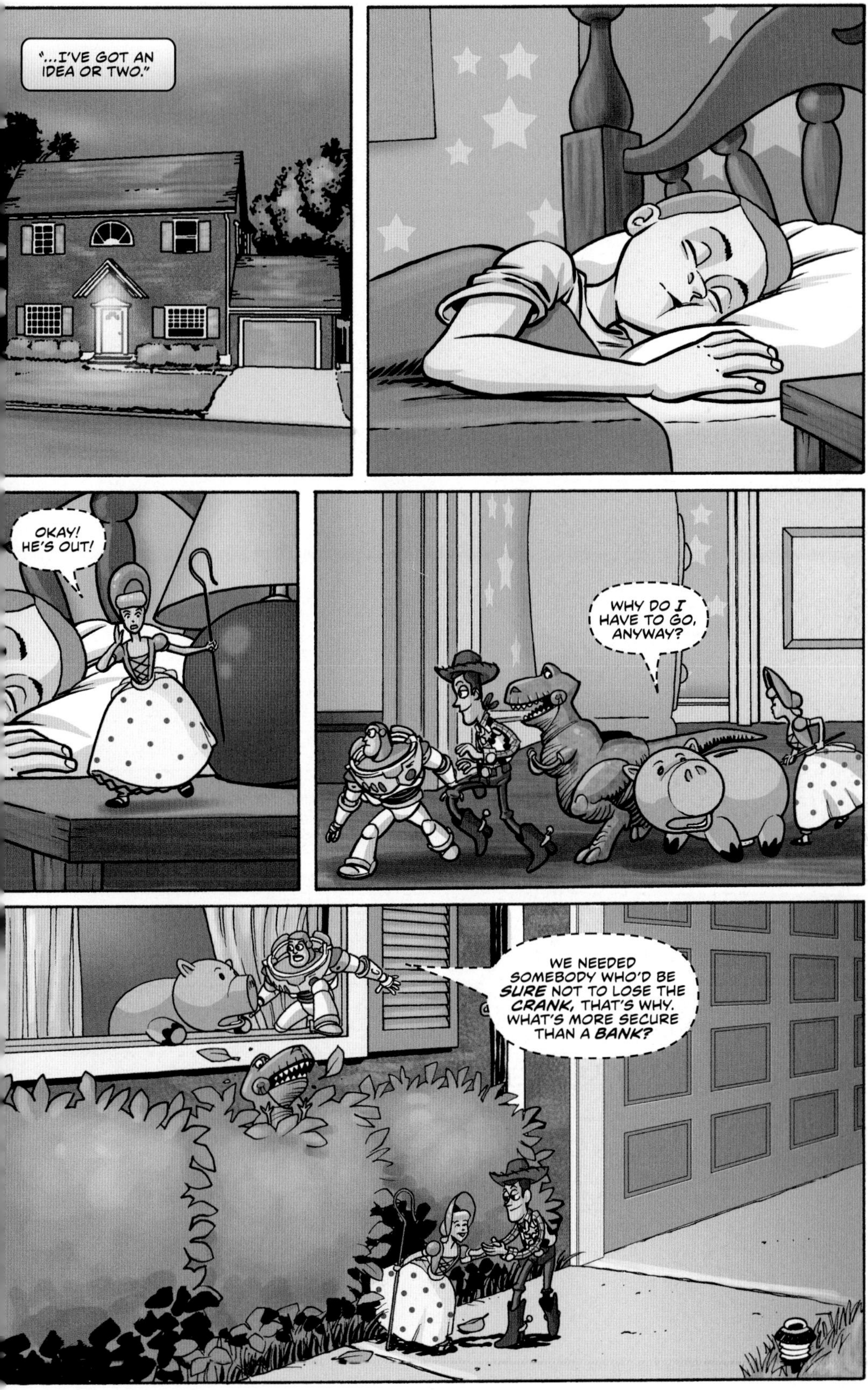

"...I'VE GOT AN IDEA OR TWO."
OKAY! HE'S OUT!
WHY DO *I* HAVE TO GO, ANYWAY?
WE NEEDED SOMEBODY WHO'D BE ***SURE*** NOT TO LOSE THE ***CRANK,*** THAT'S WHY. WHAT'S MORE SECURE THAN A ***BANK?***

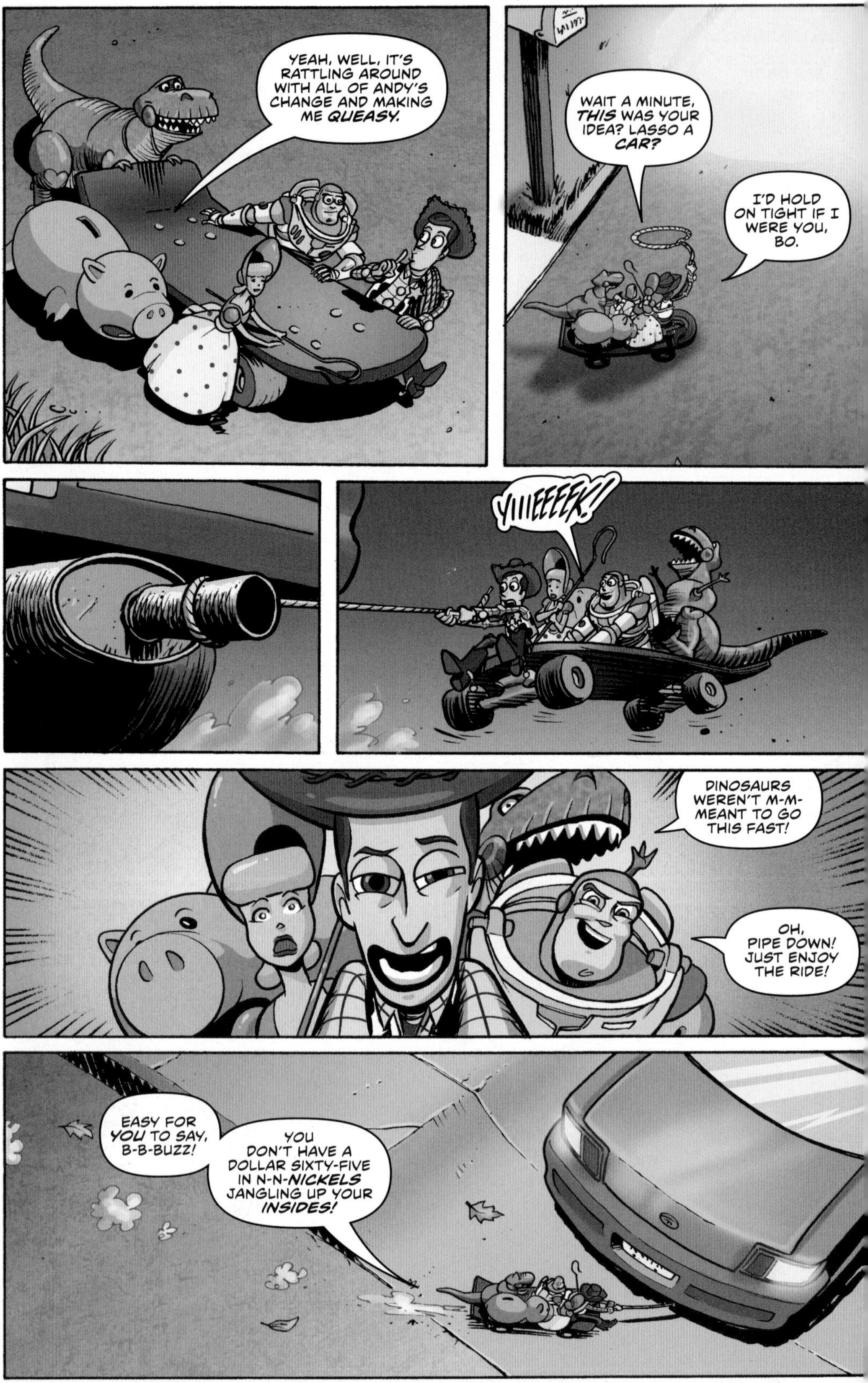
YEAH, WELL, IT'S RATTLING AROUND WITH ALL OF ANDY'S CHANGE AND MAKING ME QUEASY.
WAIT A MINUTE, THIS WAS YOUR IDEA? LASSO A CAR?
I'D HOLD ON TIGHT IF I WERE YOU, BO.
YIIIEEEEK!
DINOSAURS WEREN'T M-M-MEANT TO GO THIS FAST!
OH, PIPE DOWN! JUST ENJOY THE RIDE!
EASY FOR YOU TO SAY, B-B-BUZZ!
YOU DON'T HAVE A DOLLAR SIXTY-FIVE IN N-N-NICKELS JANGLING UP YOUR INSIDES!

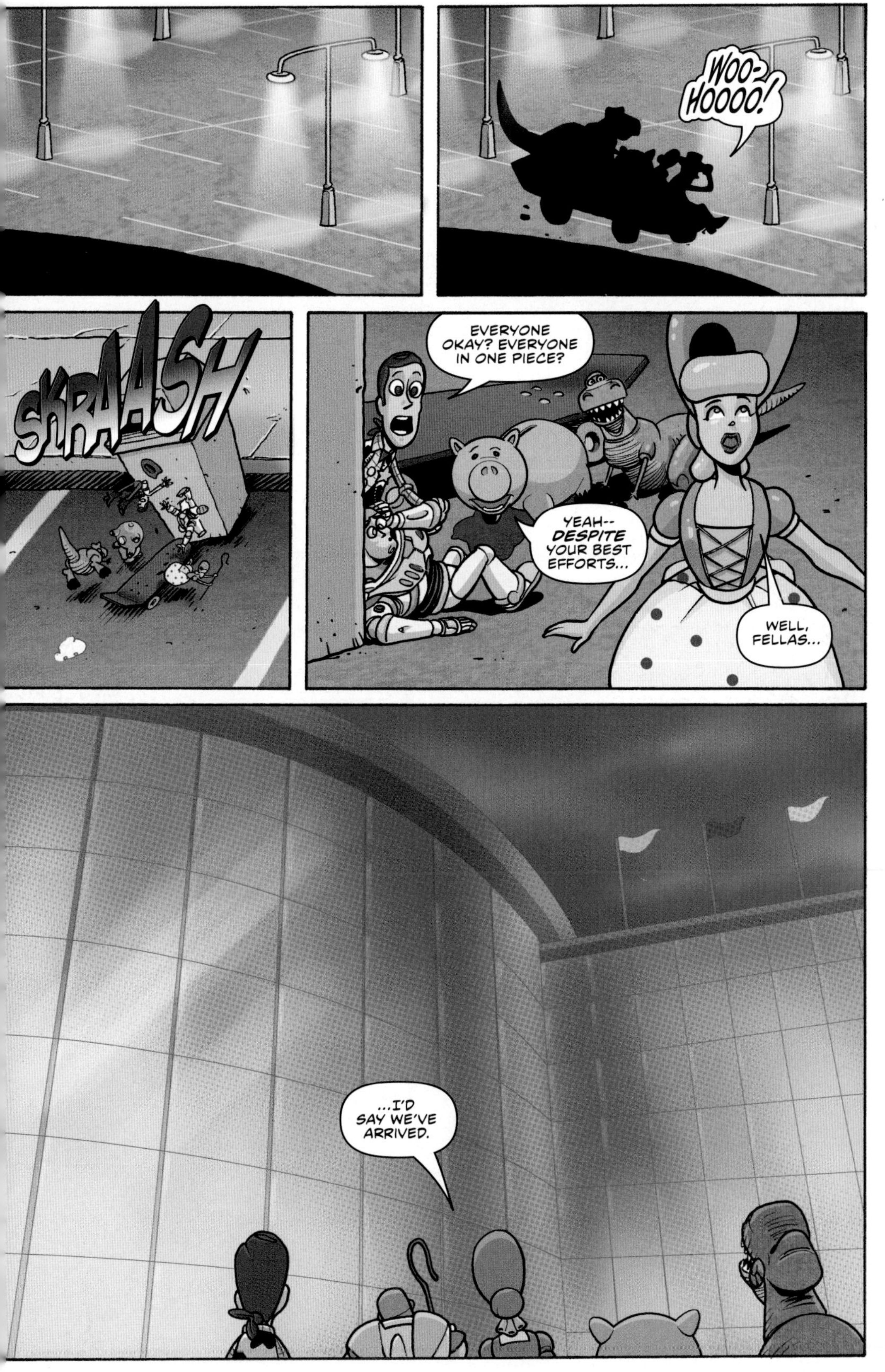
WOO-HOOOO!
SKRAASH
EVERYONE OKAY? EVERYONE IN ONE PIECE?
YEAH-- DESPITE YOUR BEST EFFORTS...
WELL, FELLAS...
...I'D SAY WE'VE ARRIVED.

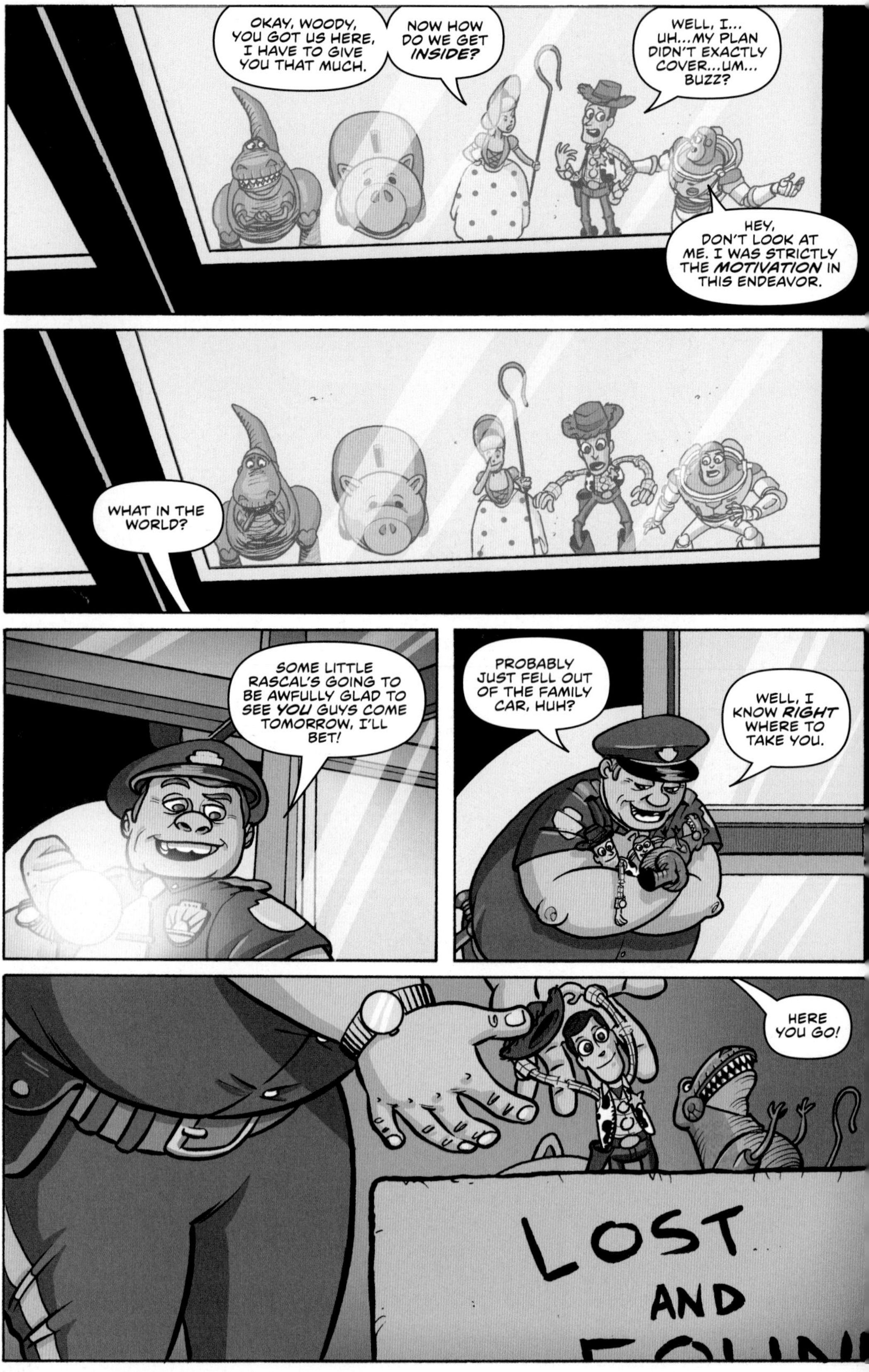
OKAY, WOODY, YOU GOT US HERE, I HAVE TO GIVE YOU THAT MUCH.
NOW HOW DO WE GET *INSIDE?*
WELL, I... UH...MY PLAN DIDN'T EXACTLY COVER...UM... BUZZ?
HEY, DON'T LOOK AT ME. I WAS STRICTLY THE *MOTIVATION* IN THIS ENDEAVOR.
WHAT IN THE WORLD?
SOME LITTLE RASCAL'S GOING TO BE AWFULLY GLAD TO SEE *YOU* GUYS COME TOMORROW, I'LL BET!
PROBABLY JUST FELL OUT OF THE FAMILY CAR, HUH?
WELL, I KNOW *RIGHT* WHERE TO TAKE YOU.
HERE YOU GO!
LOST
AND

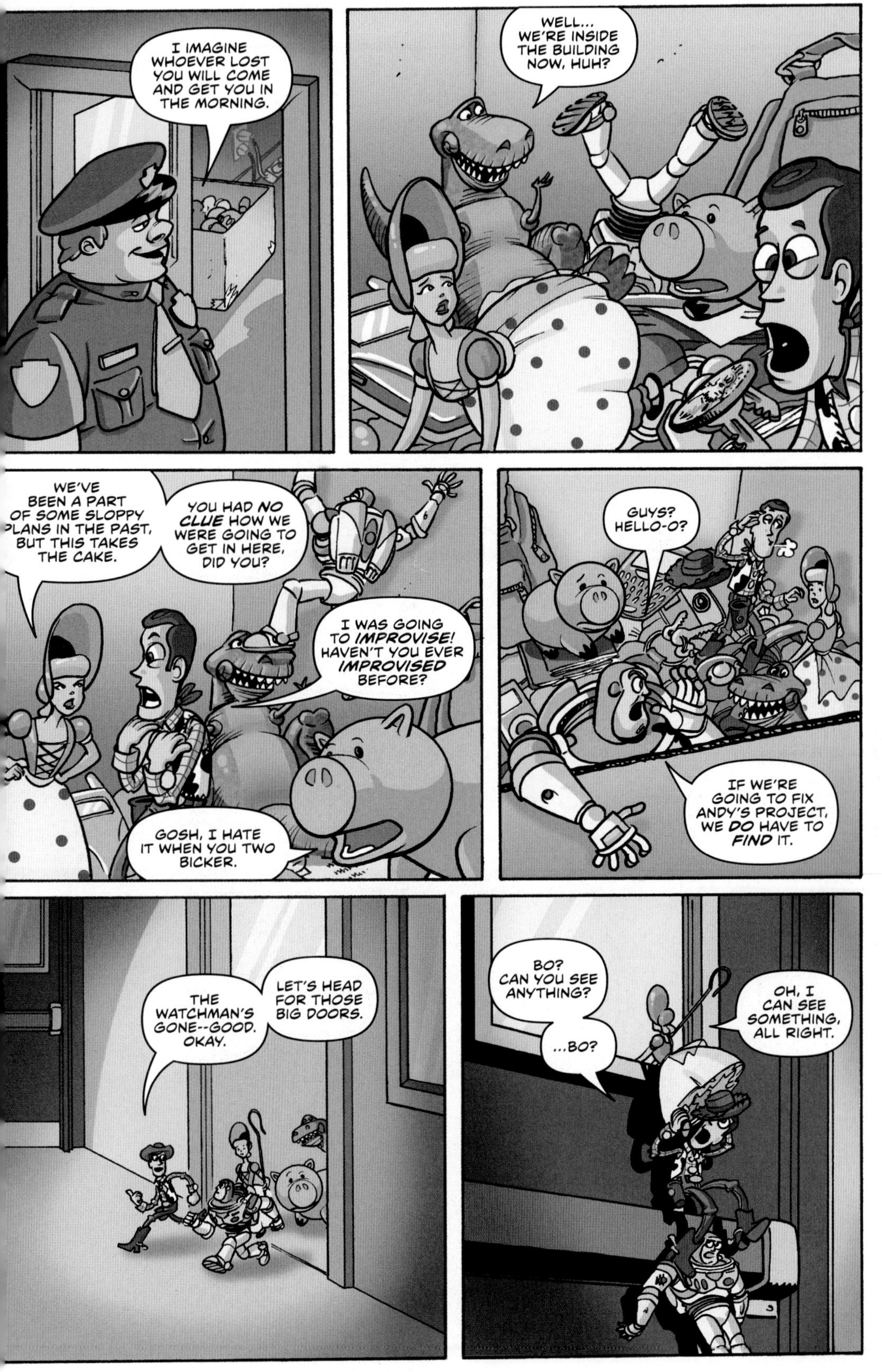

I IMAGINE WHOEVER LOST YOU WILL COME AND GET YOU IN THE MORNING.
WELL... WE'RE INSIDE THE BUILDING NOW, HUH?
WE'VE BEEN A PART OF SOME SLOPPY PLANS IN THE PAST, BUT THIS TAKES THE CAKE.
YOU HAD NO CLUE HOW WE WERE GOING TO GET IN HERE, DID YOU?
I WAS GOING TO IMPROVISE! HAVEN'T YOU EVER IMPROVISED BEFORE?
GOSH, I HATE IT WHEN YOU TWO BICKER.
GUYS? HELLO-O?
IF WE'RE GOING TO FIX ANDY'S PROJECT, WE DO HAVE TO FIND IT.
THE WATCHMAN'S GONE--GOOD. OKAY.
LET'S HEAD FOR THOSE BIG DOORS.
BO? CAN YOU SEE ANYTHING?
...BO?
OH, I CAN SEE SOMETHING, ALL RIGHT.

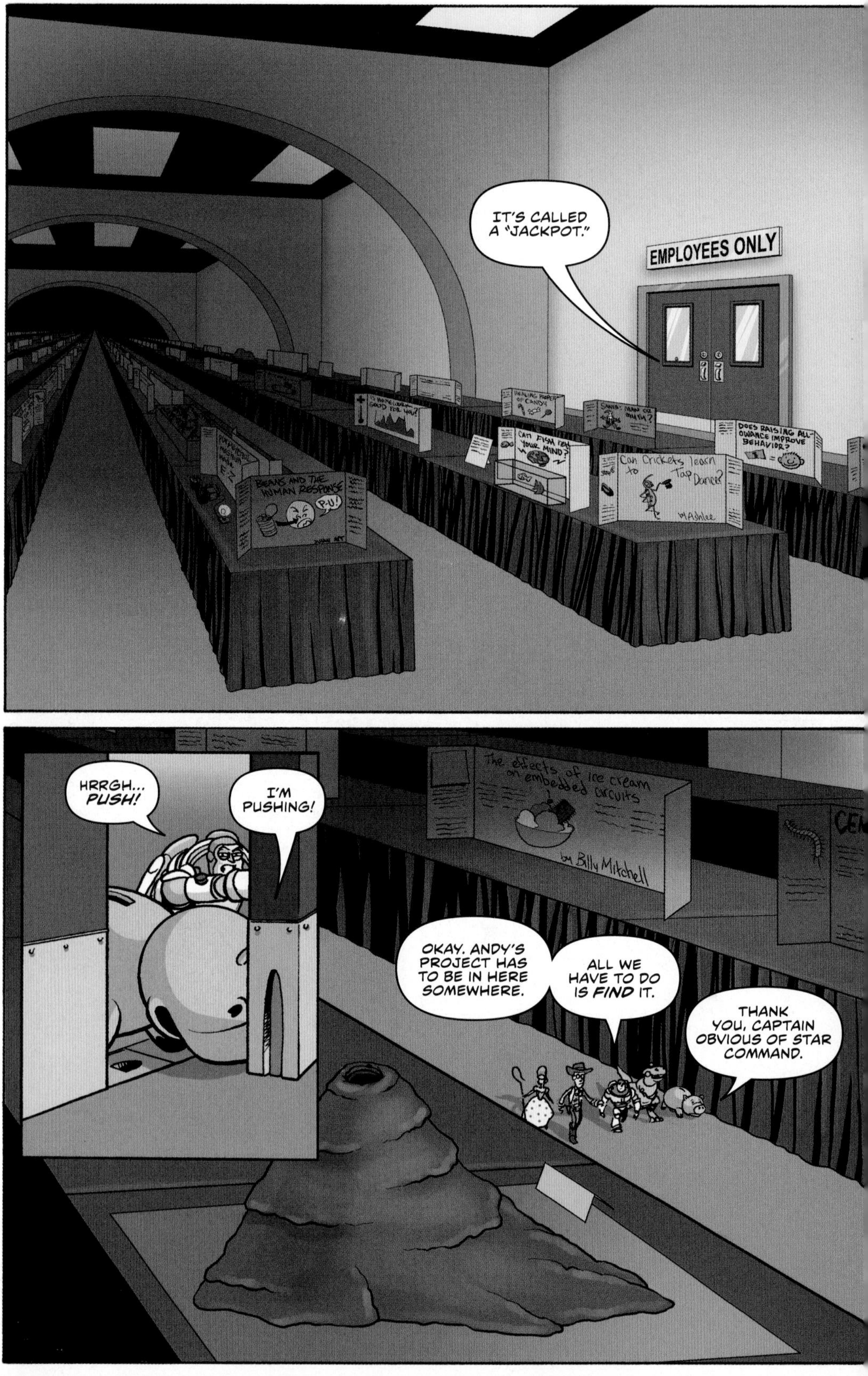
IT'S CALLED A "JACKPOT."
EMPLOYEES ONLY
BEANS AND THE HUMAN RESPONSE
P-U!
CAN FISH READ YOUR MIND?
Can Crickets learn to Tap Dance?
MAshlee
DOES RAISING ALLOWANCE IMPROVE BEHAVIOR?
HRRGH... *PUSH!*
I'M PUSHING!
The effects of ice cream on embedded circuits
by Billy Mitchell
OKAY. ANDY'S PROJECT HAS TO BE IN HERE SOMEWHERE.
ALL WE HAVE TO DO IS *FIND* IT.
THANK YOU, CAPTAIN OBVIOUS OF STAR COMMAND.

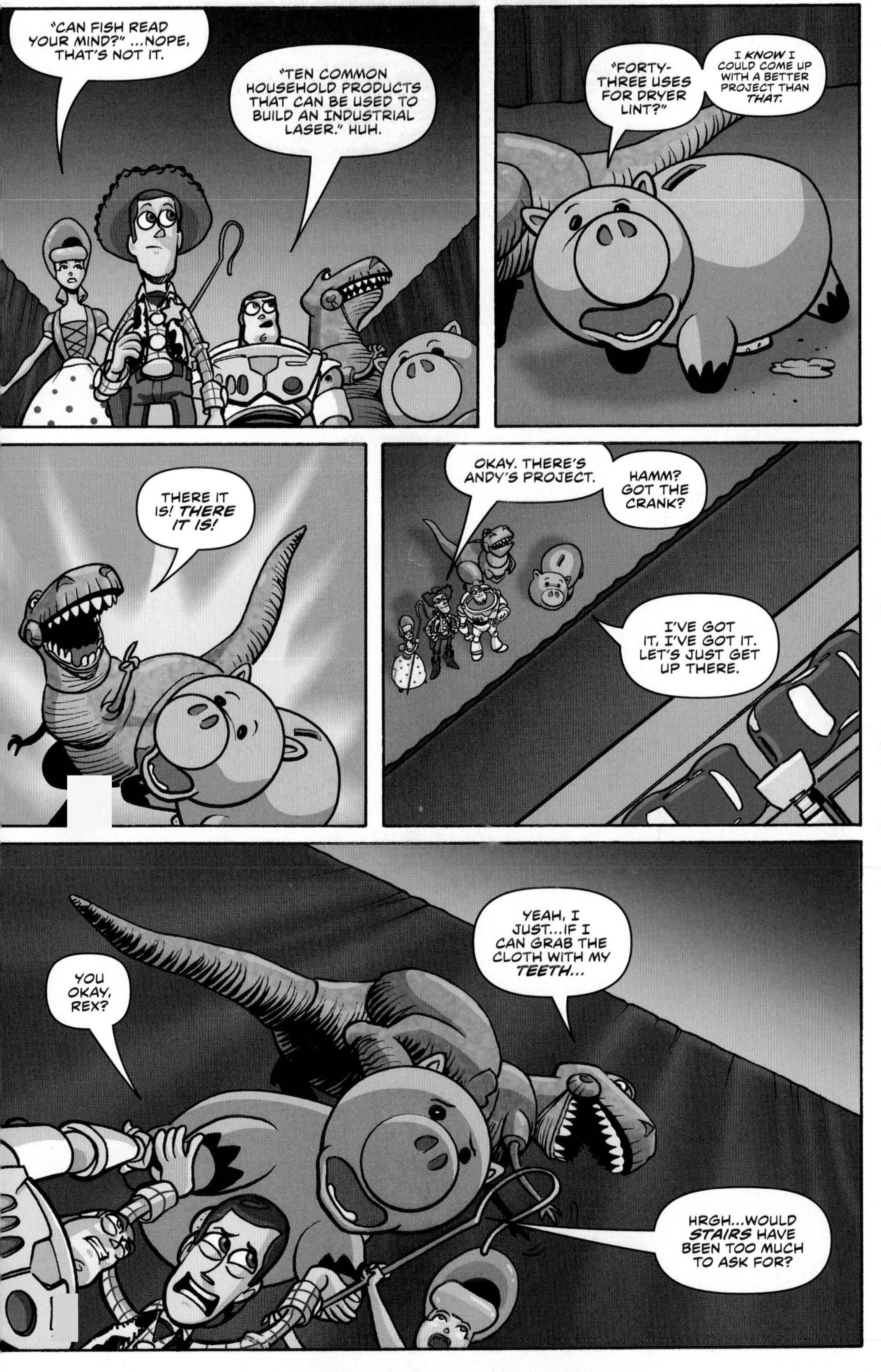
"CAN FISH READ YOUR MIND?" ...NOPE, THAT'S NOT IT.
"TEN COMMON HOUSEHOLD PRODUCTS THAT CAN BE USED TO BUILD AN INDUSTRIAL LASER." HUH.
"FORTY-THREE USES FOR DRYER LINT?"
I *KNOW* I COULD COME UP WITH A BETTER PROJECT THAN *THAT.*
THERE IT IS! *THERE IT IS!*
OKAY. THERE'S ANDY'S PROJECT.
HAMM? GOT THE CRANK?
I'VE GOT IT, I'VE GOT IT. LET'S JUST GET UP THERE.
YOU OKAY, REX?
YEAH, I JUST...IF I CAN GRAB THE CLOTH WITH MY *TEETH...*
HRGH...WOULD *STAIRS* HAVE BEEN TOO MUCH TO ASK FOR?

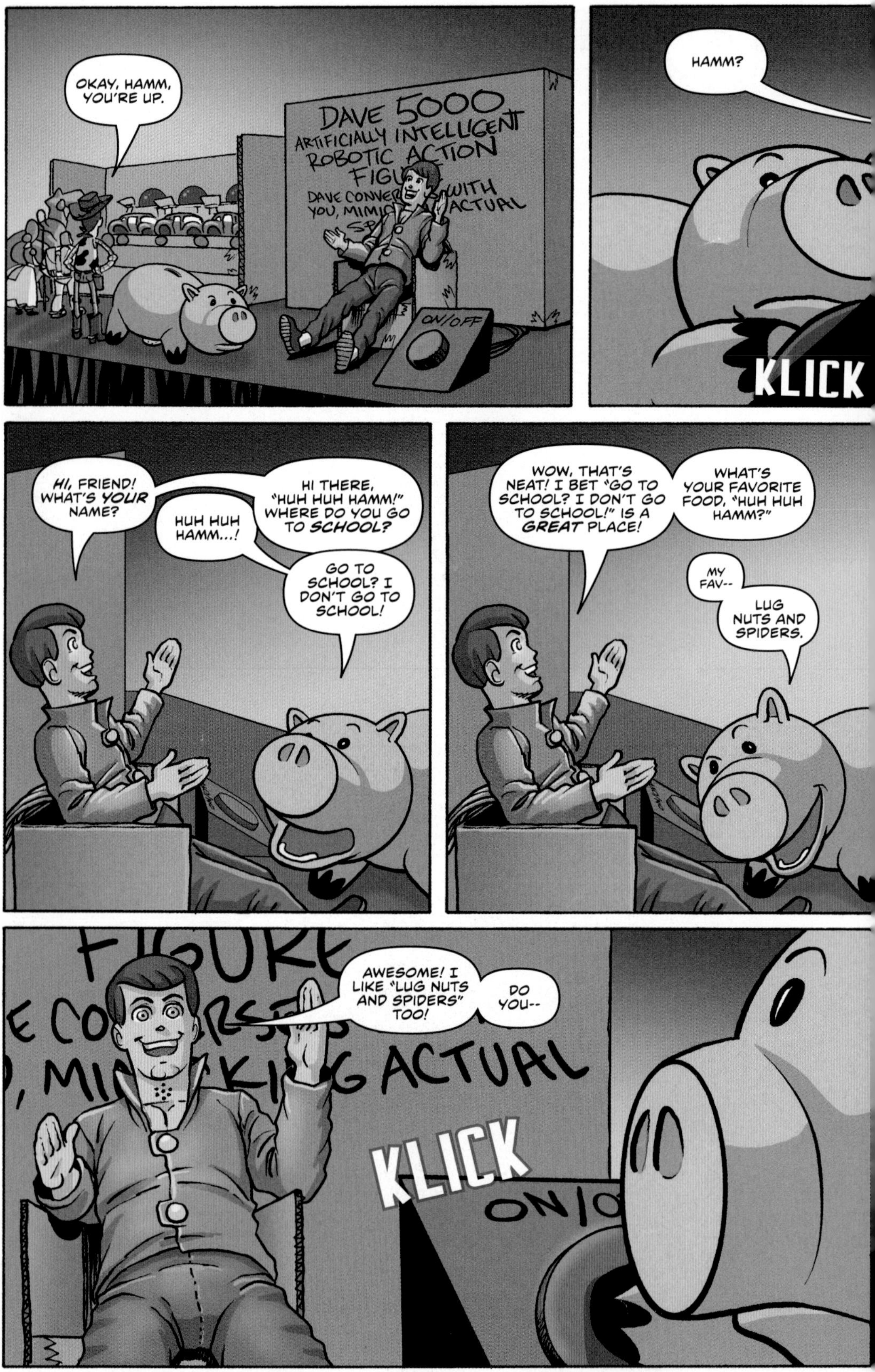
OKAY, HAMM, YOU'RE UP.
DAVE 5000 ARTIFICIALLY INTELLIGENT ROBOTIC ACTION FIGU
DAVE CONVER WITH YOU, MIMI ACTUAL
ON/OFF
HAMM?
KLICK
HI, FRIEND! WHAT'S YOUR NAME?
HUH HUH HAMM...!
HI THERE, "HUH HUH HAMM!" WHERE DO YOU GO TO SCHOOL?
GO TO SCHOOL? I DON'T GO TO SCHOOL!
WOW, THAT'S NEAT! I BET "GO TO SCHOOL? I DON'T GO TO SCHOOL!" IS A GREAT PLACE!
WHAT'S YOUR FAVORITE FOOD, "HUH HUH HAMM?"
MY FAV--
LUG NUTS AND SPIDERS.
FIGURE
AWESOME! I LIKE "LUG NUTS AND SPIDERS" TOO!
DO YOU--
ACTUAL
KLICK
ON/O

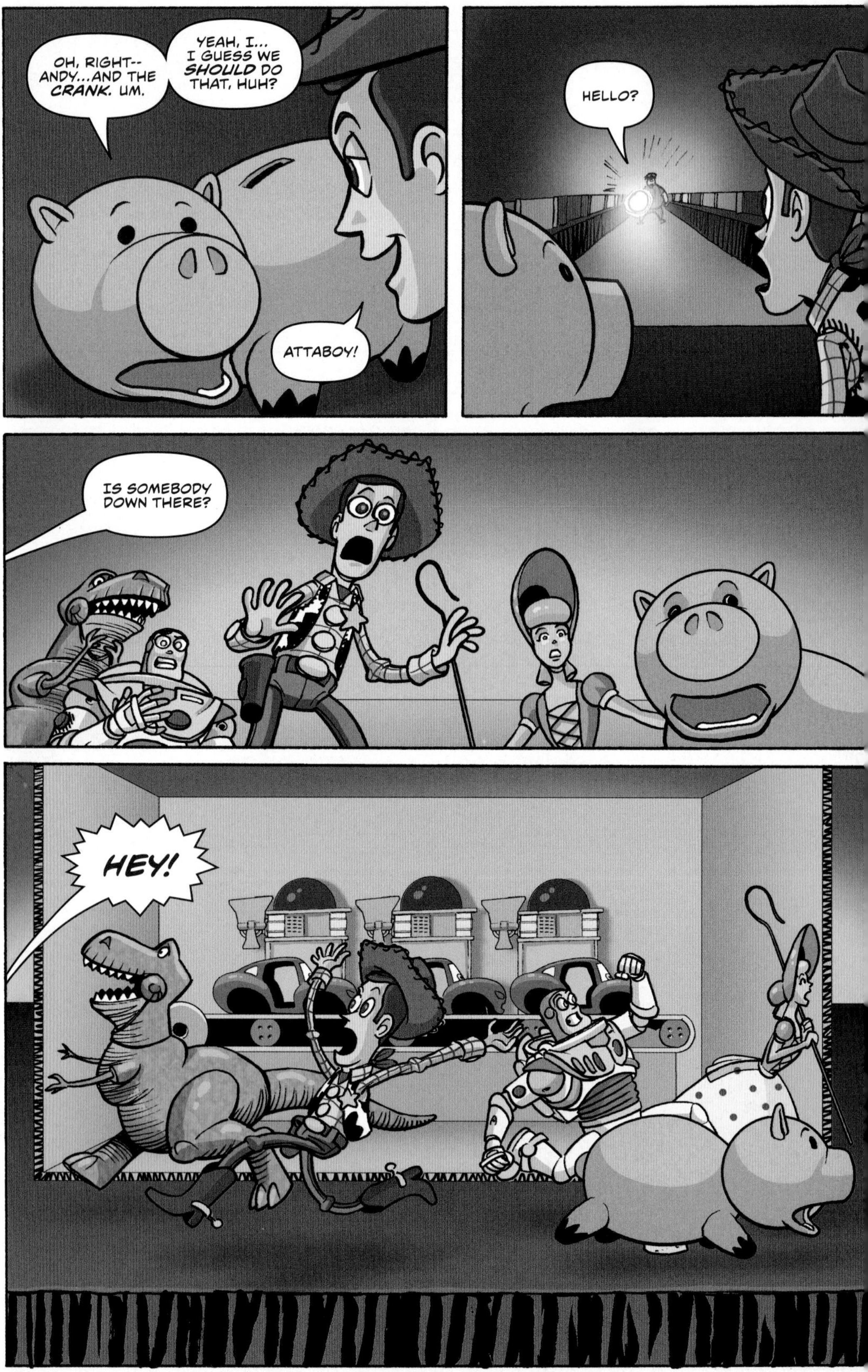
OH, RIGHT-- ANDY...AND THE CRANK. UM.
YEAH, I... I GUESS WE SHOULD DO THAT, HUH?
ATTABOY!
HELLO?
IS SOMEBODY DOWN THERE?
HEY!

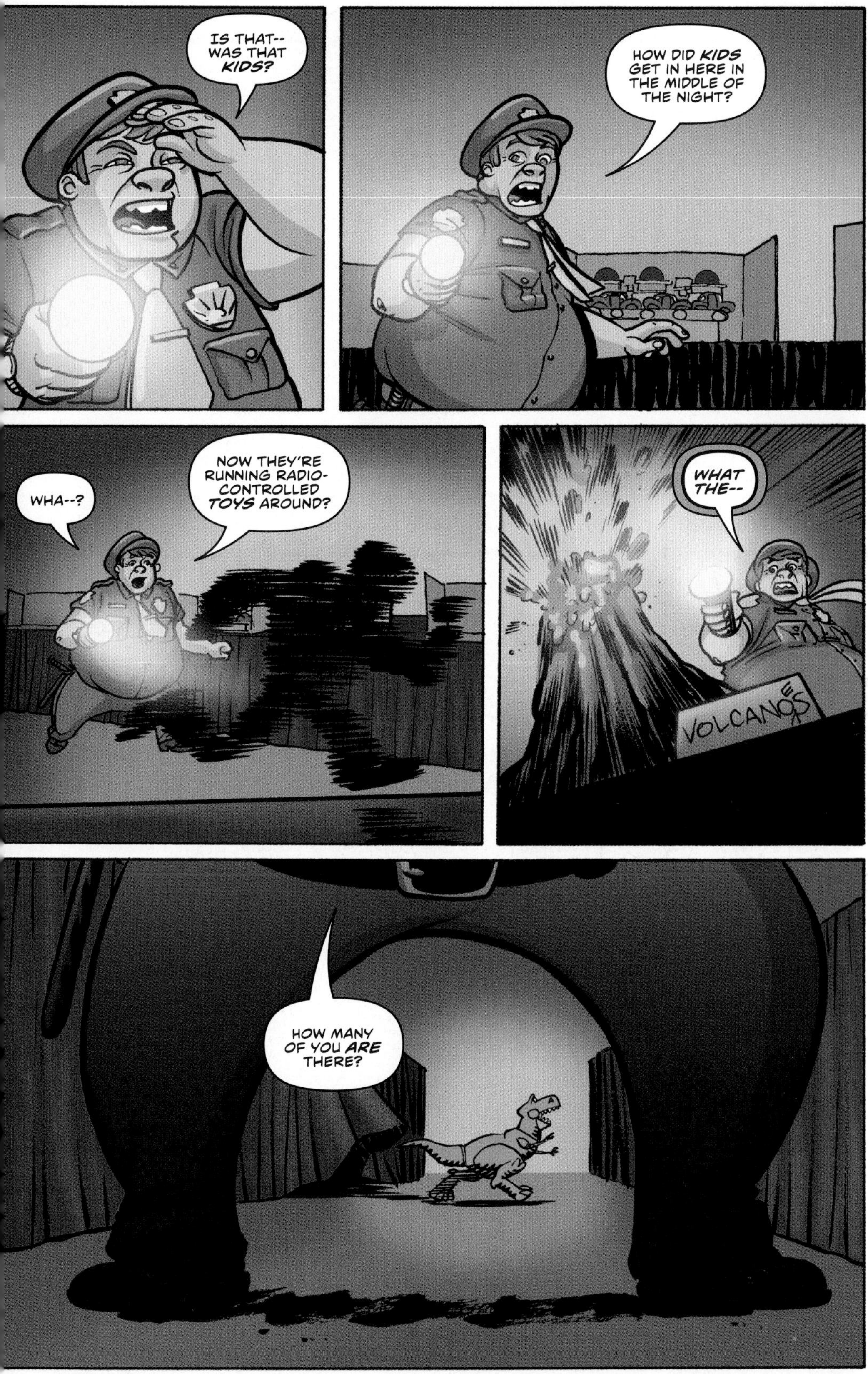
IS THAT-- WAS THAT KIDS?
HOW DID KIDS GET IN HERE IN THE MIDDLE OF THE NIGHT?
WHA--?
NOW THEY'RE RUNNING RADIO-CONTROLLED TOYS AROUND?
WHAT THE--
VOLCANOES
HOW MANY OF YOU ARE THERE?

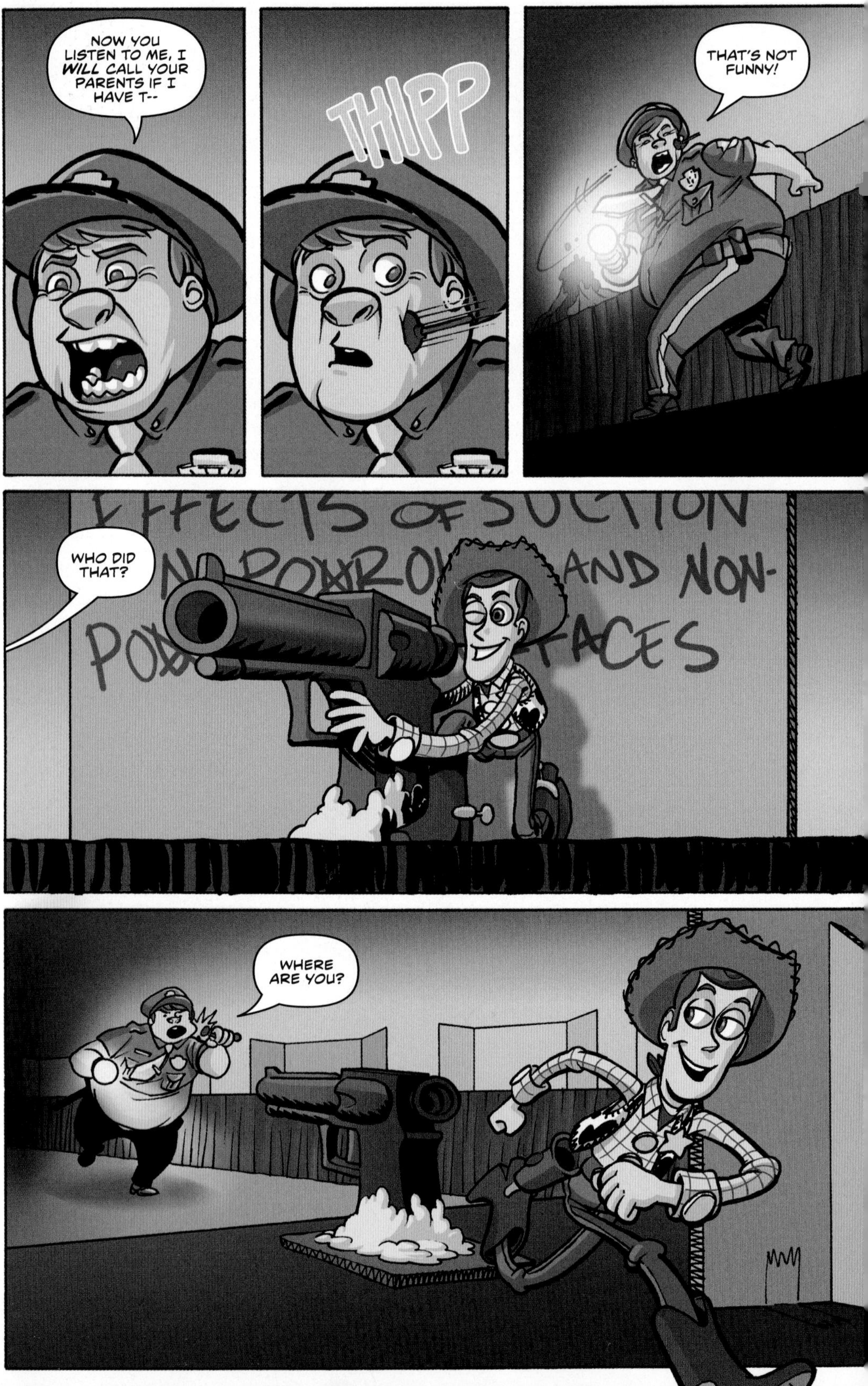
NOW YOU LISTEN TO ME, I *WILL* CALL YOUR PARENTS IF I HAVE T--
THIPP
THAT'S NOT FUNNY!
EFFECTS OF SUCTION
AND NON-
WHO DID THAT?
WHERE ARE YOU?

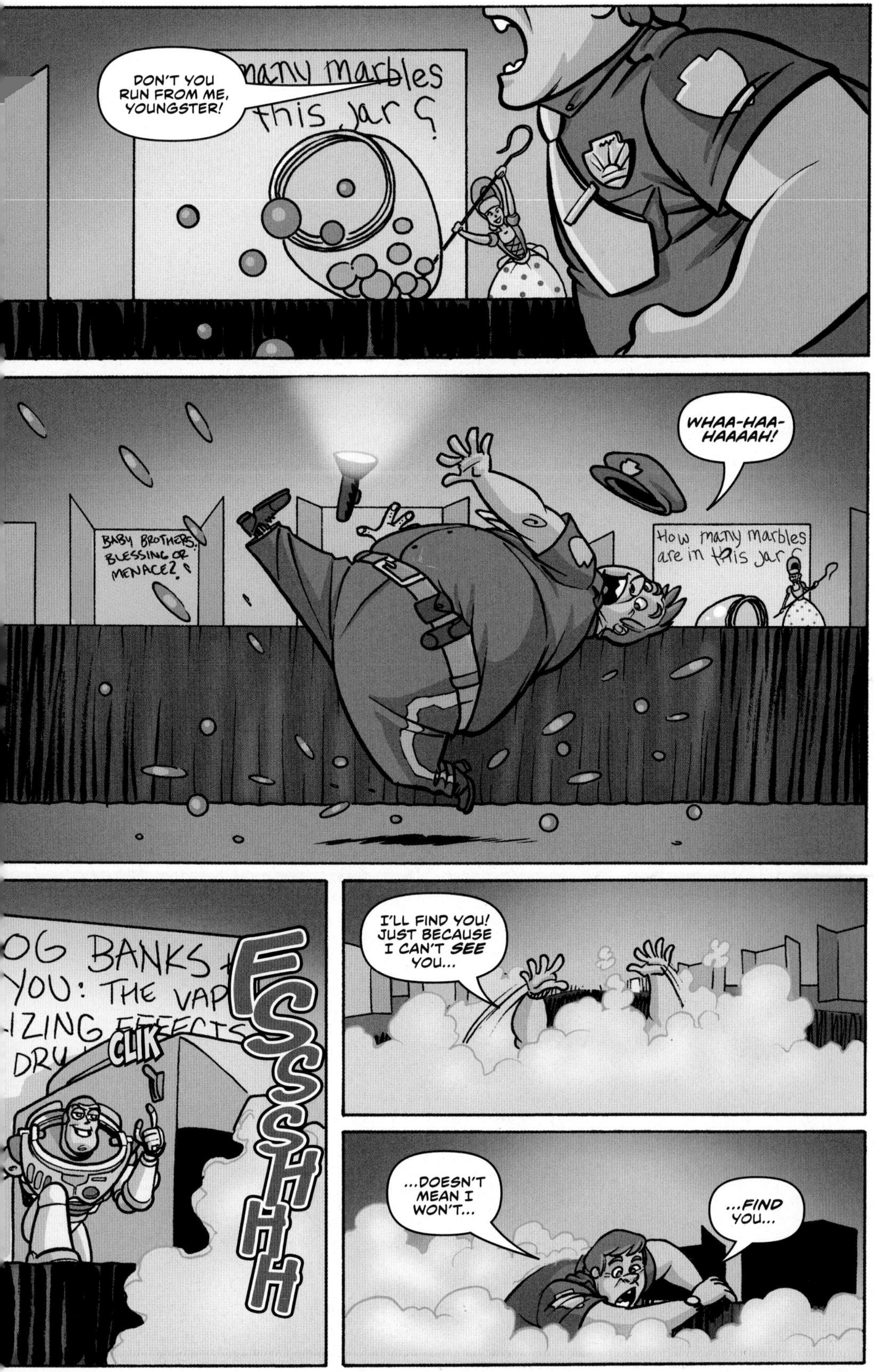
DON'T YOU RUN FROM ME, YOUNGSTER!
many marbles
this jar ?
WHAA-HAA-HAAAAH!
BABY BROTHERS: BLESSING OR MENACE?
How many marbles are in this jar ?
OG BANKS
YOU: THE VAP
IZING EFFECTS
CLIK
FSSSHHHH
I'LL FIND YOU! JUST BECAUSE I CAN'T SEE YOU...
...DOESN'T MEAN I WON'T...
...FIND YOU...

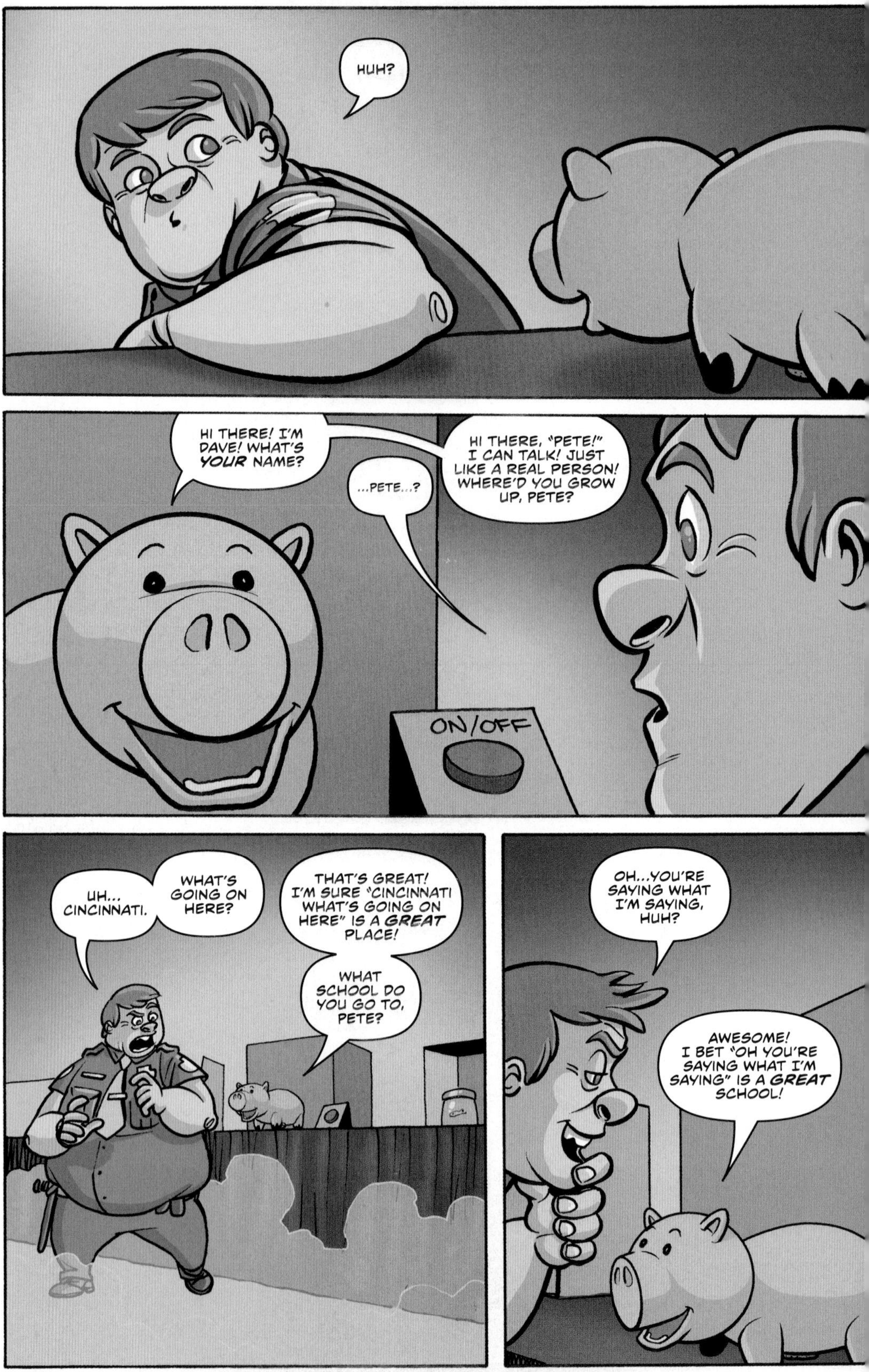
HUH?
HI THERE! I'M DAVE! WHAT'S *YOUR* NAME?
...PETE...?
HI THERE, "PETE!" I CAN TALK! JUST LIKE A REAL PERSON! WHERE'D YOU GROW UP, PETE?
ON/OFF
UH... CINCINNATI.
WHAT'S GOING ON HERE?
THAT'S GREAT! I'M SURE "CINCINNATI WHAT'S GOING ON HERE" IS A *GREAT* PLACE!
WHAT SCHOOL DO YOU GO TO, PETE?
OH...YOU'RE SAYING WHAT I'M SAYING, HUH?
AWESOME! I BET "OH YOU'RE SAYING WHAT I'M SAYING" IS A *GREAT* SCHOOL!

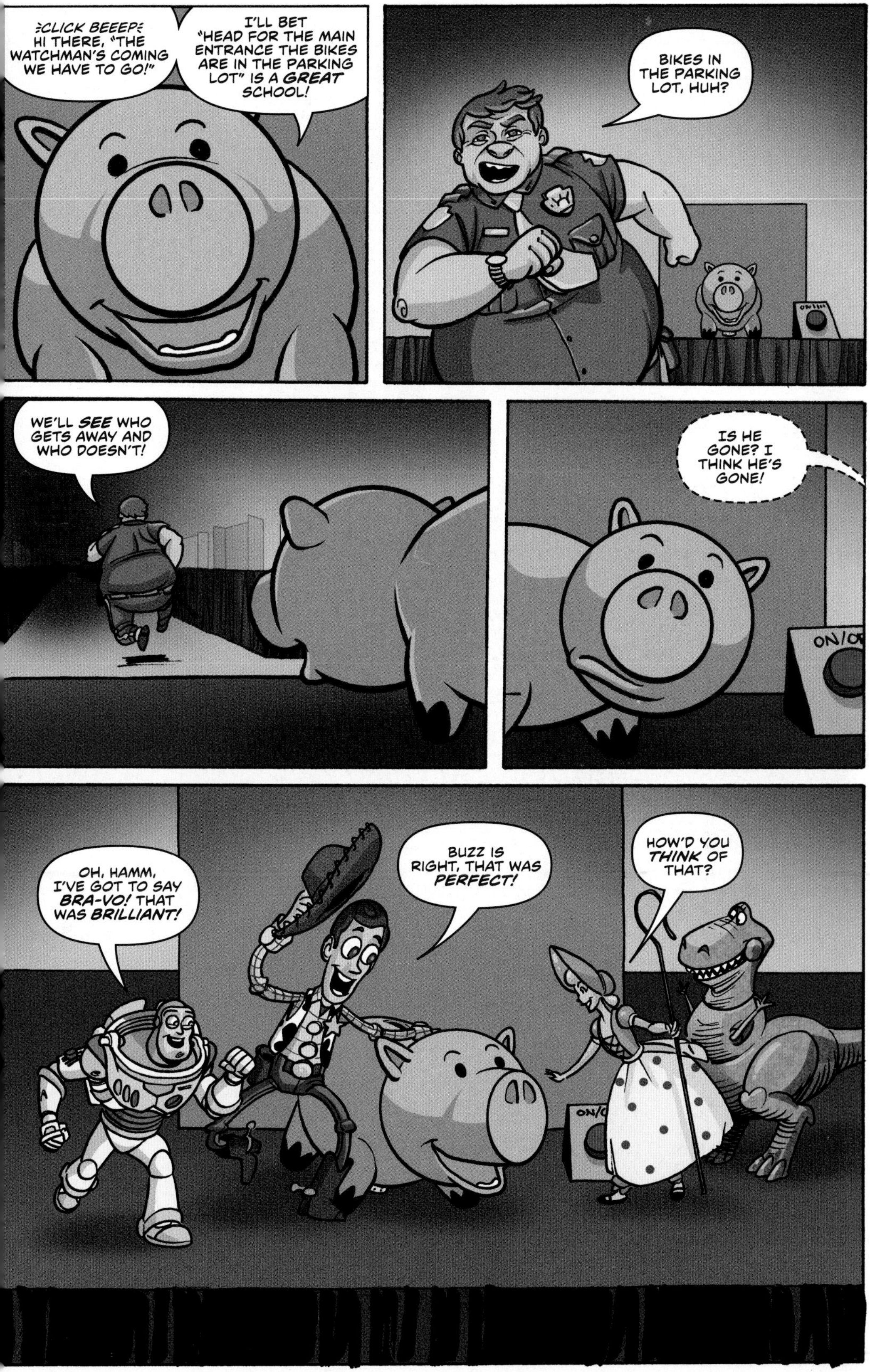

≡CLICK BEEEP≡ HI THERE, "THE WATCHMAN'S COMING WE HAVE TO GO!"
I'LL BET "HEAD FOR THE MAIN ENTRANCE THE BIKES ARE IN THE PARKING LOT" IS A *GREAT* SCHOOL!
BIKES IN THE PARKING LOT, HUH?
ON/OFF
WE'LL *SEE* WHO GETS AWAY AND WHO DOESN'T!
IS HE GONE? I THINK HE'S GONE!
OH, HAMM, I'VE GOT TO SAY *BRA-VO!* THAT WAS *BRILLIANT!*
BUZZ IS RIGHT, THAT WAS *PERFECT!*
HOW'D YOU *THINK* OF THAT?

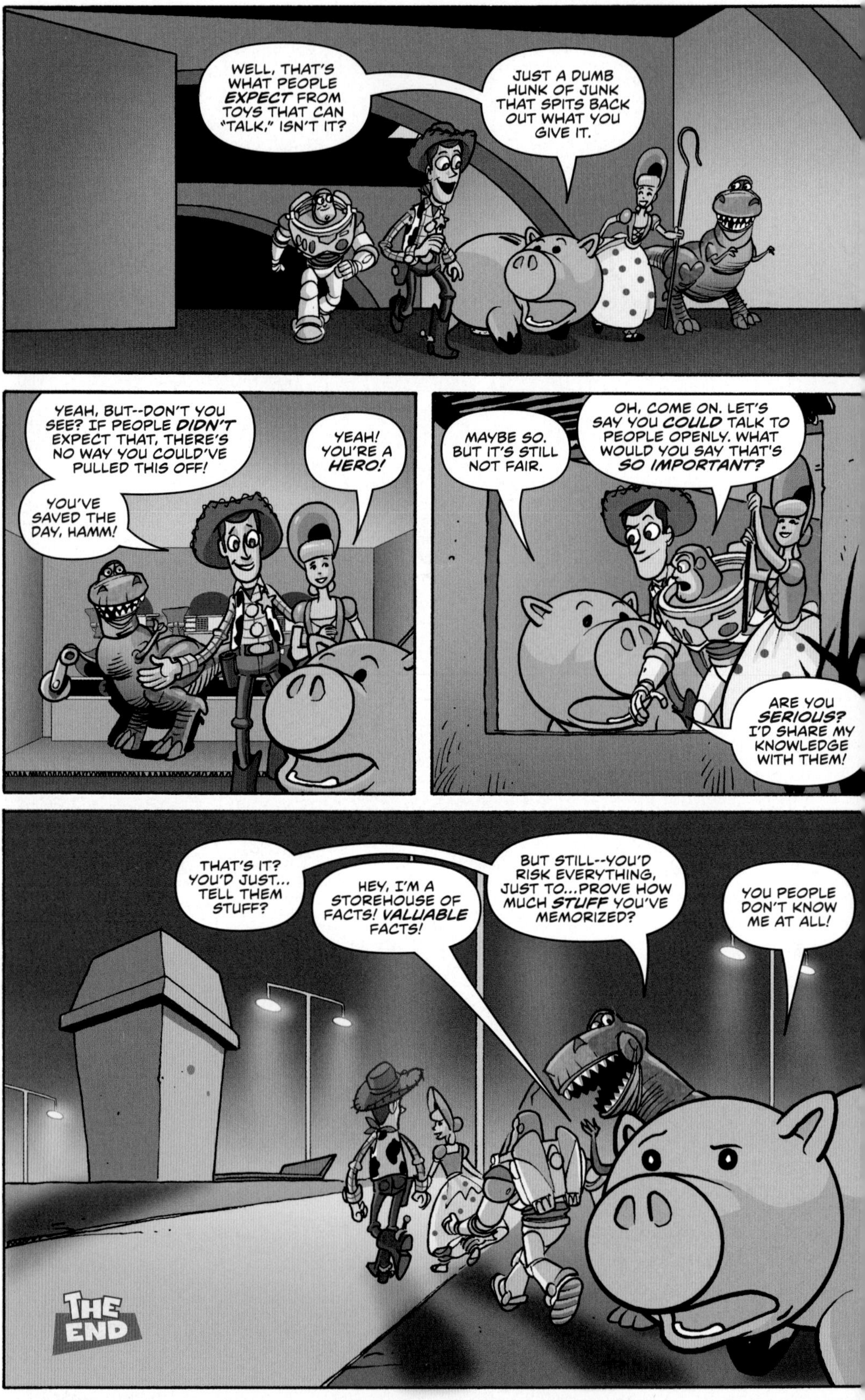
WELL, THAT'S WHAT PEOPLE *EXPECT* FROM TOYS THAT CAN "TALK," ISN'T IT?
JUST A DUMB HUNK OF JUNK THAT SPITS BACK OUT WHAT YOU GIVE IT.
YEAH, BUT--DON'T YOU SEE? IF PEOPLE *DIDN'T* EXPECT THAT, THERE'S NO WAY YOU COULD'VE PULLED THIS OFF!
YOU'VE SAVED THE DAY, HAMM!
YEAH! YOU'RE A *HERO!*
MAYBE SO. BUT IT'S STILL NOT FAIR.
OH, COME ON. LET'S SAY YOU *COULD* TALK TO PEOPLE OPENLY. WHAT WOULD YOU SAY THAT'S *SO IMPORTANT?*
ARE YOU *SERIOUS?* I'D SHARE MY KNOWLEDGE WITH THEM!
THAT'S IT? YOU'D JUST... TELL THEM STUFF?
HEY, I'M A STOREHOUSE OF FACTS! *VALUABLE* FACTS!
BUT STILL--YOU'D RISK EVERYTHING, JUST TO...PROVE HOW MUCH *STUFF* YOU'VE MEMORIZED?
YOU PEOPLE DON'T KNOW ME AT ALL!
THE END

CHAPTER THREE

A Dog's Life

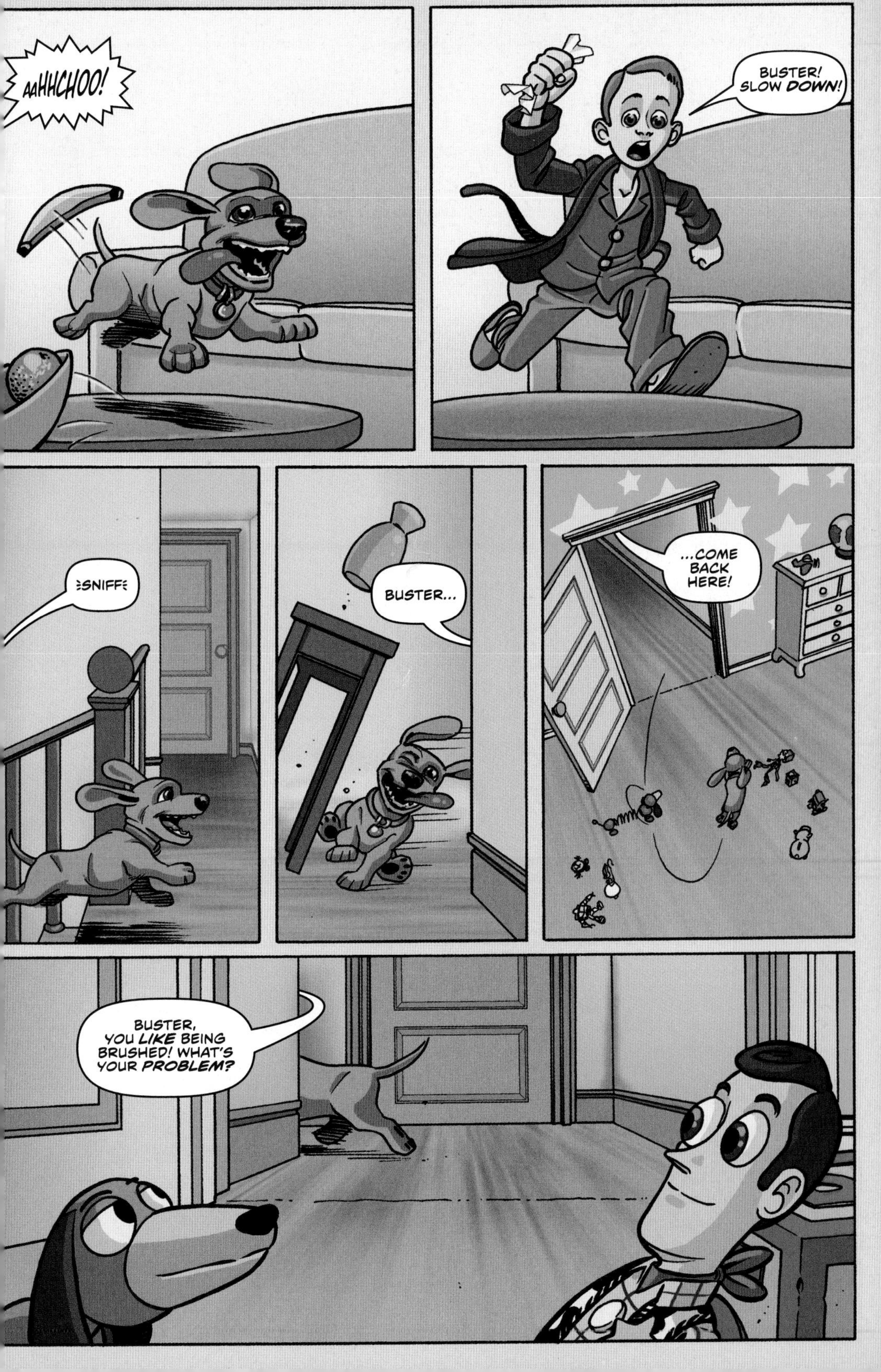
AAHHCHOO!
BUSTER! SLOW DOWN!
SNIFF
BUSTER...
...COME BACK HERE!
BUSTER, YOU LIKE BEING BRUSHED! WHAT'S YOUR PROBLEM?

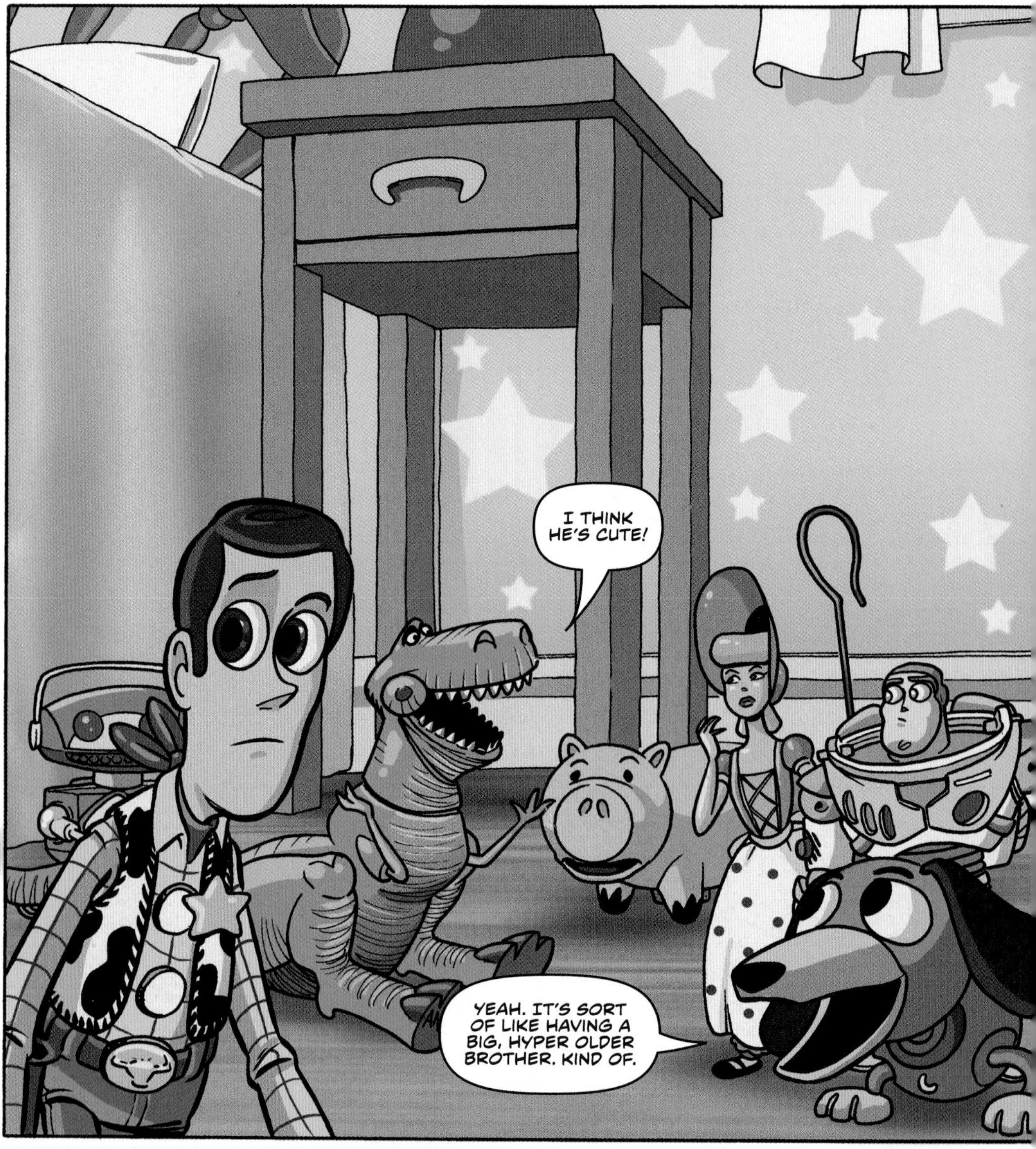
I THINK HE'S CUTE!
YEAH. IT'S SORT OF LIKE HAVING A BIG, HYPER OLDER BROTHER. KIND OF.

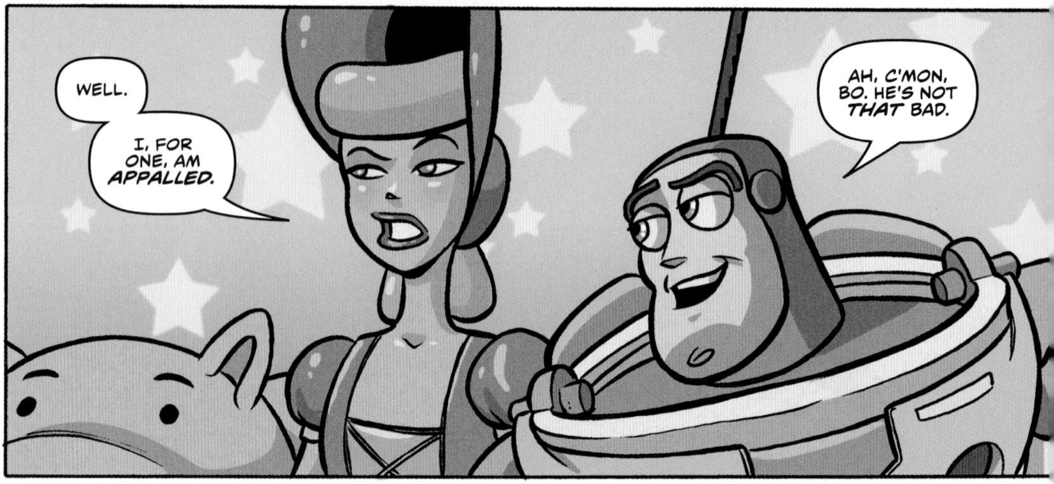
WELL.
I, FOR ONE, AM *APPALLED*.
AH, C'MON, BO. HE'S NOT *THAT* BAD.

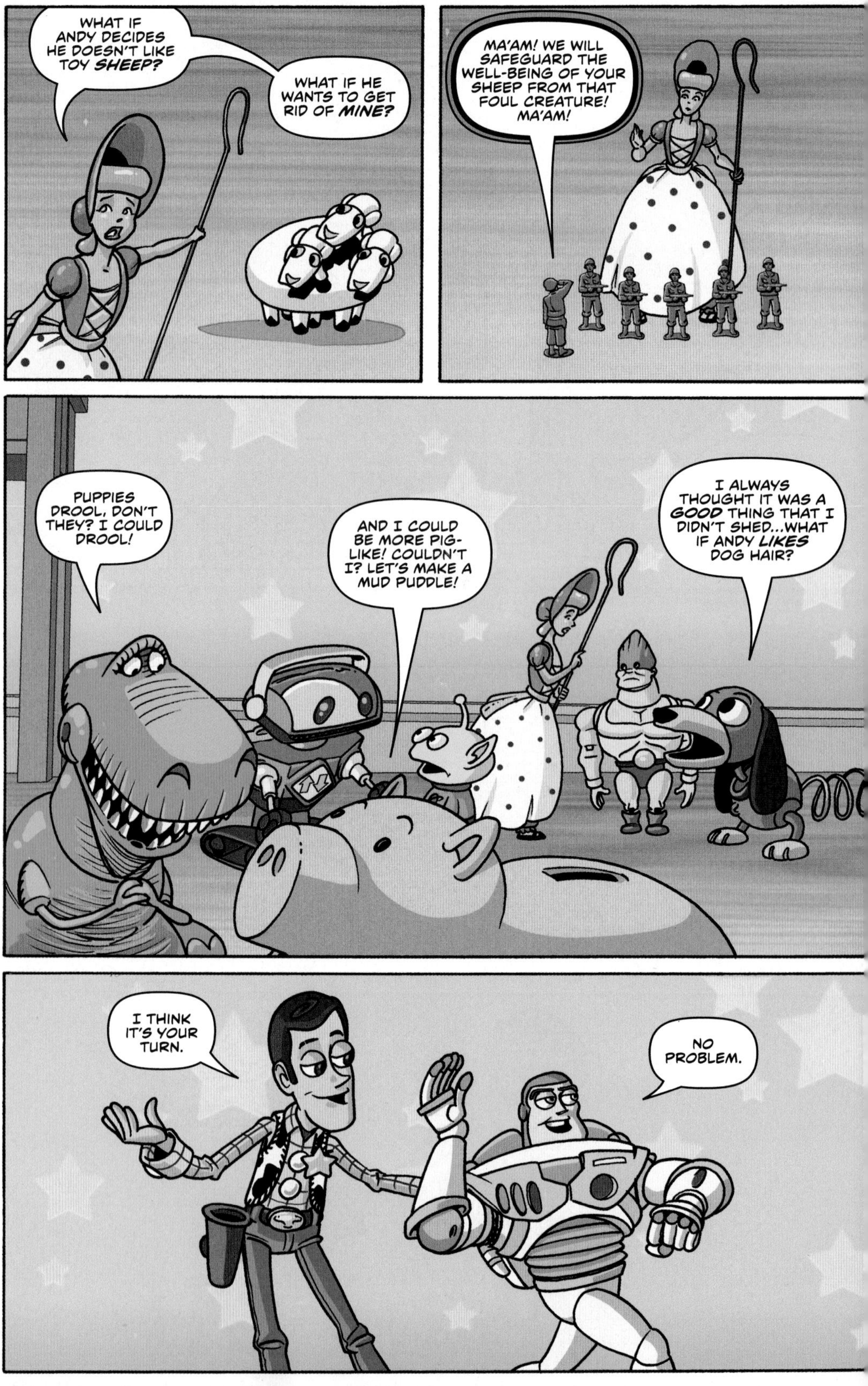
WHAT IF ANDY DECIDES HE DOESN'T LIKE TOY *SHEEP?*
WHAT IF HE WANTS TO GET RID OF *MINE?*
MA'AM! WE WILL SAFEGUARD THE WELL-BEING OF YOUR SHEEP FROM THAT FOUL CREATURE! MA'AM!
PUPPIES DROOL, DON'T THEY? I COULD DROOL!
AND I COULD BE MORE PIG-LIKE! COULDN'T I? LET'S MAKE A MUD PUDDLE!
I ALWAYS THOUGHT IT WAS A *GOOD* THING THAT I DIDN'T SHED...WHAT IF ANDY *LIKES* DOG HAIR?
I THINK IT'S YOUR TURN.
NO PROBLEM.

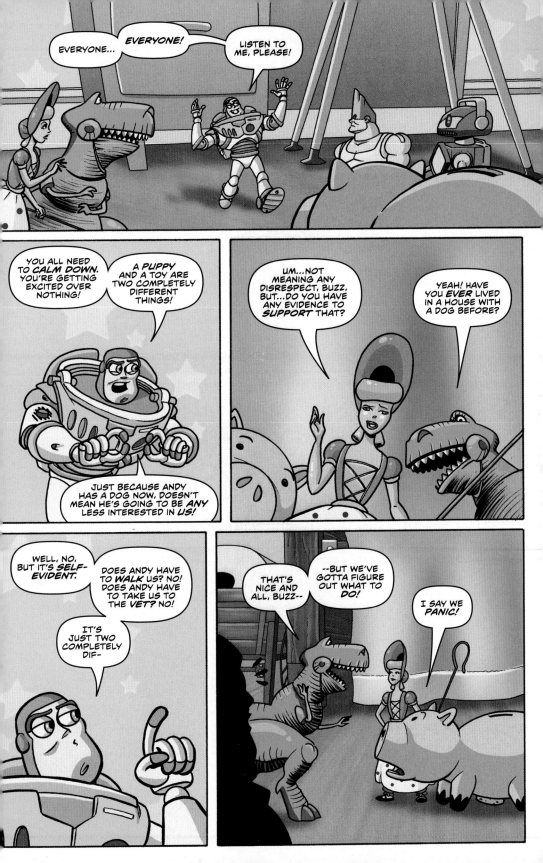

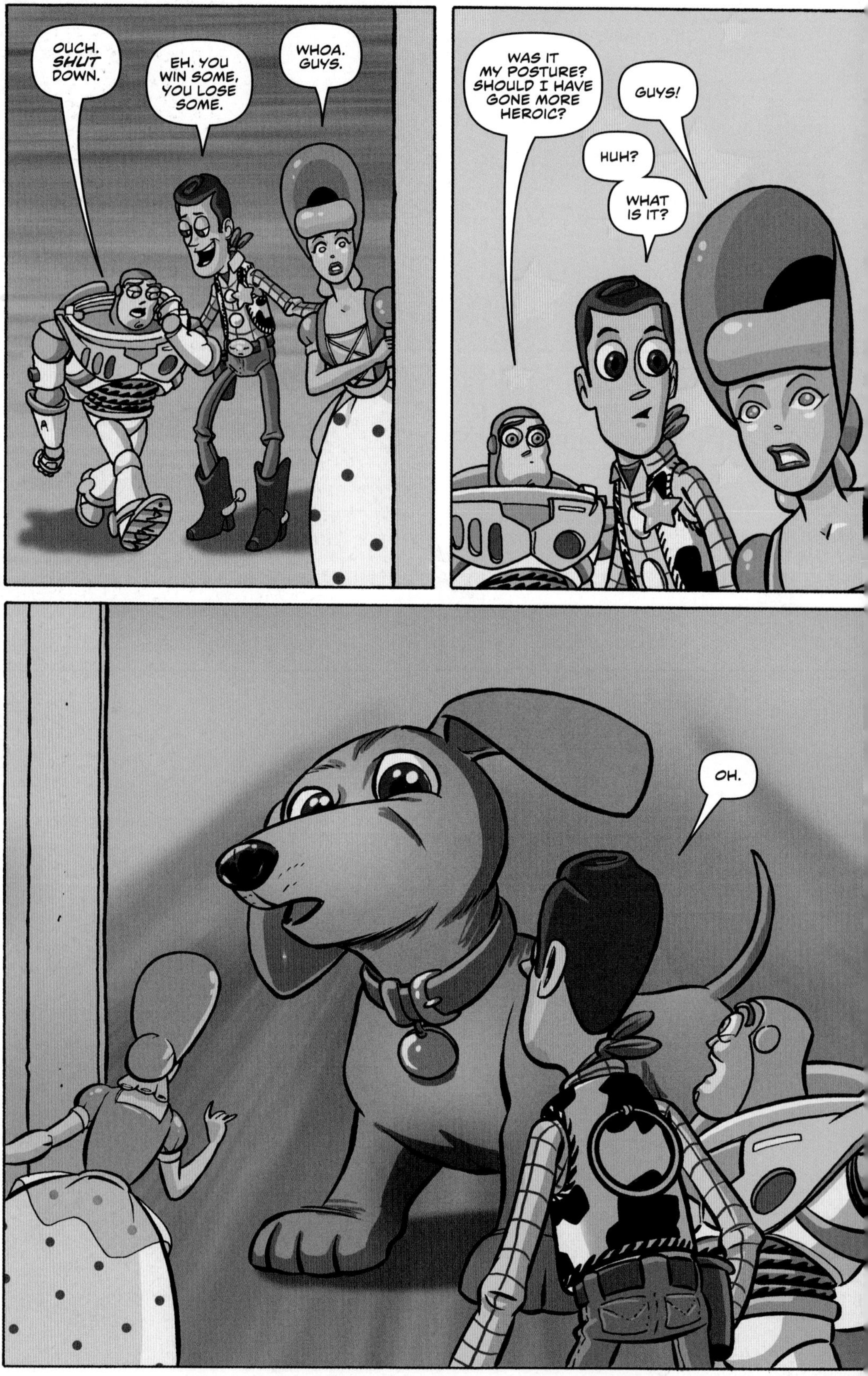

OUCH. SHUT DOWN.
EH. YOU WIN SOME, YOU LOSE SOME.
WHOA. GUYS.
WAS IT MY POSTURE? SHOULD I HAVE GONE MORE HEROIC?
GUYS!
HUH?
WHAT IS IT?
OH.

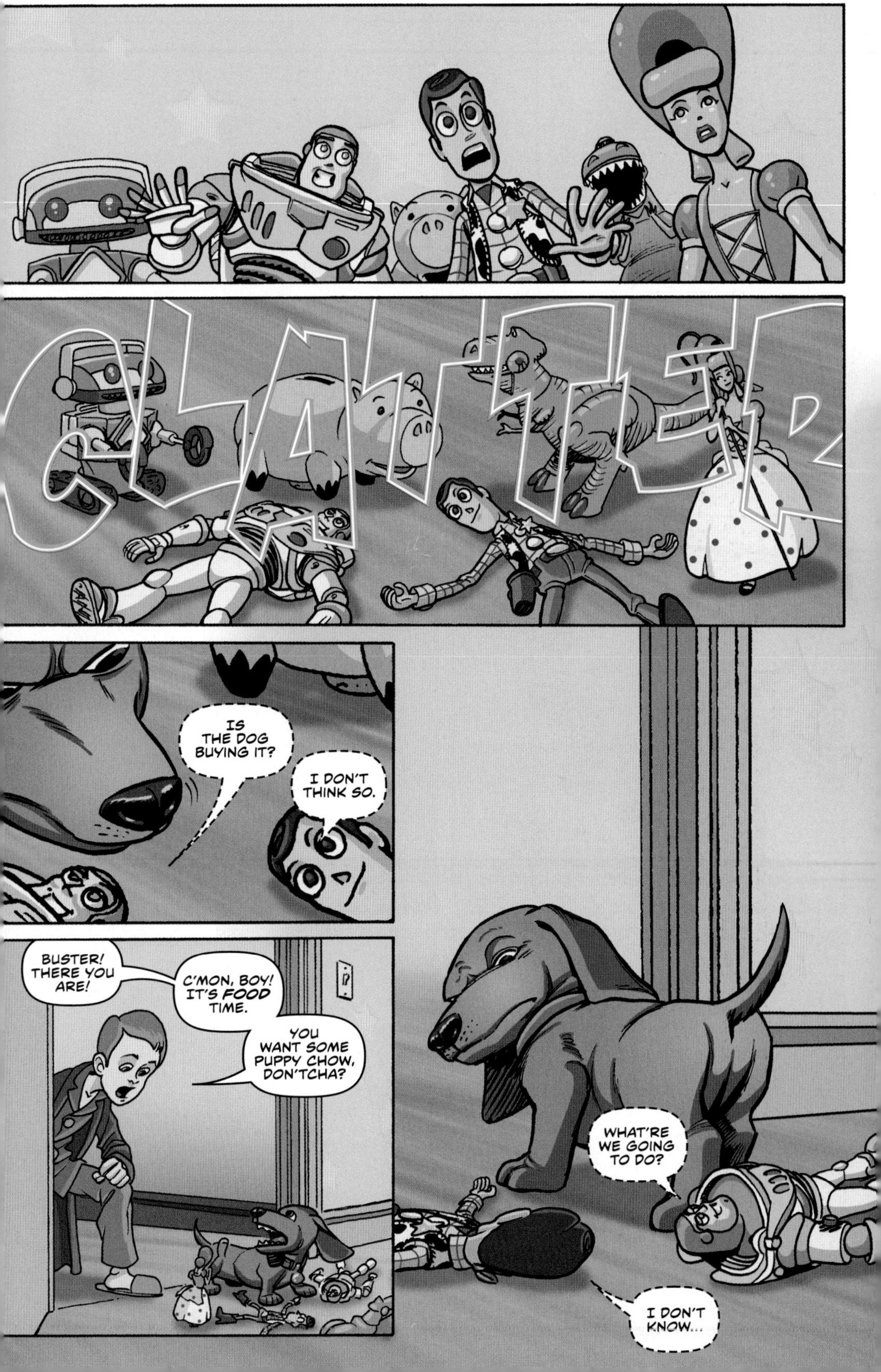
CLATTER
IS THE DOG BUYING IT?
I DON'T THINK SO.
BUSTER! THERE YOU ARE!
C'MON, BOY! IT'S FOOD TIME.
YOU WANT SOME PUPPY CHOW, DON'TCHA?
WHAT'RE WE GOING TO DO?
I DON'T KNOW...

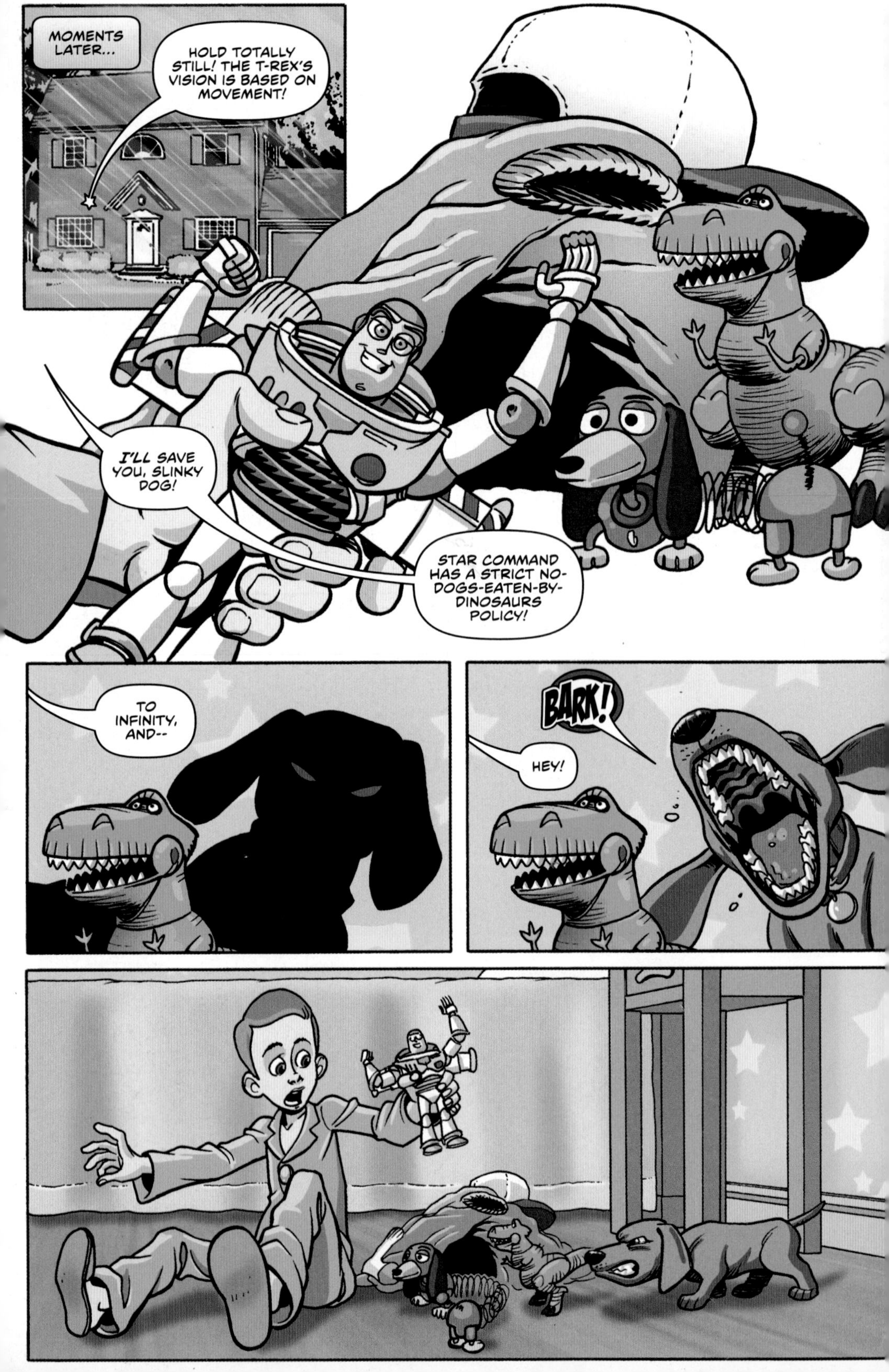
MOMENTS LATER...
HOLD TOTALLY STILL! THE T-REX'S VISION IS BASED ON MOVEMENT!
I'LL SAVE YOU, SLINKY DOG!
STAR COMMAND HAS A STRICT NO-DOGS-EATEN-BY-DINOSAURS POLICY!
TO INFINITY, AND--
BARK!
HEY!

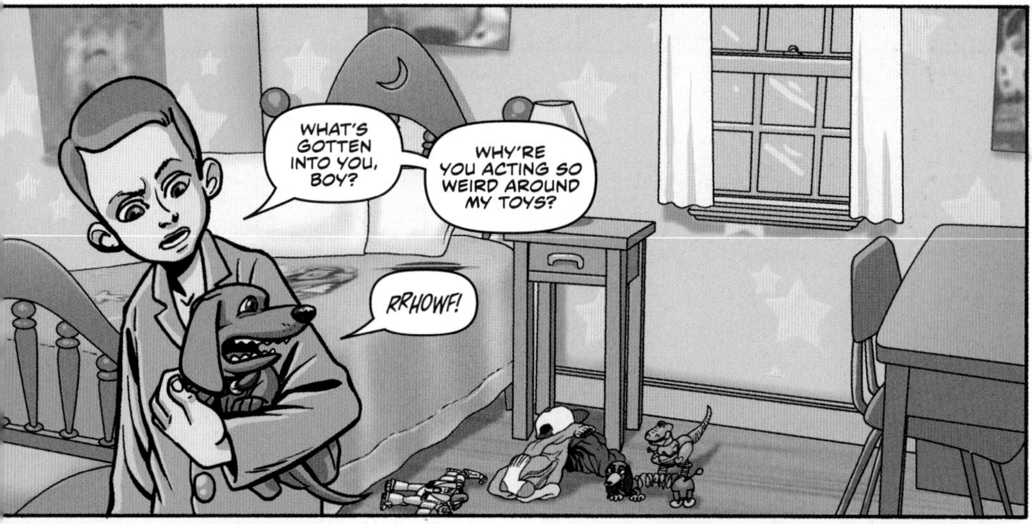
WHAT'S GOTTEN INTO YOU, BOY?
WHY'RE YOU ACTING SO WEIRD AROUND MY TOYS?
RRHOWF!

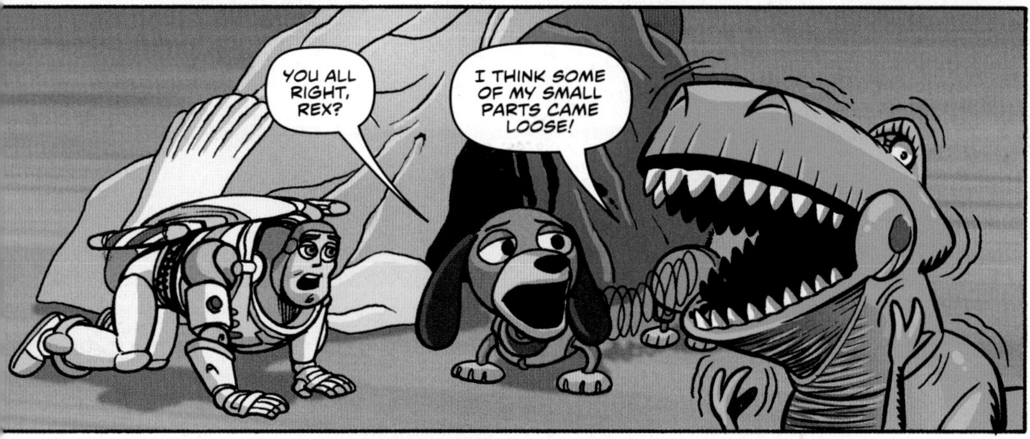
YOU ALL RIGHT, REX?
I THINK SOME OF MY SMALL PARTS CAME LOOSE!

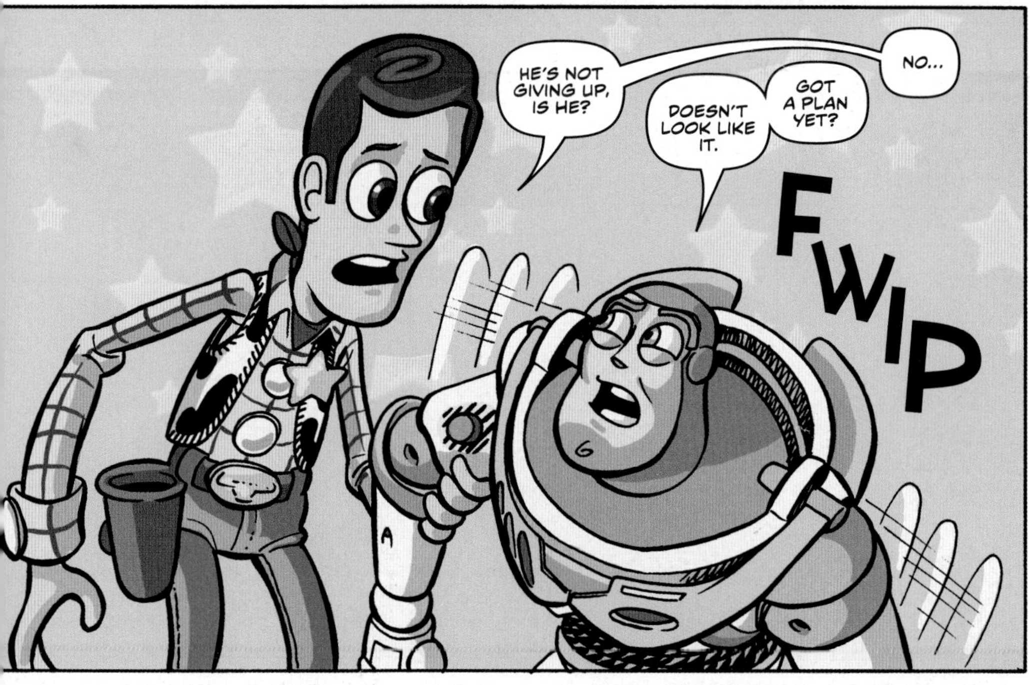
HE'S NOT GIVING UP, IS HE?
NO...
DOESN'T LOOK LIKE IT.
GOT A PLAN YET?
FWIP

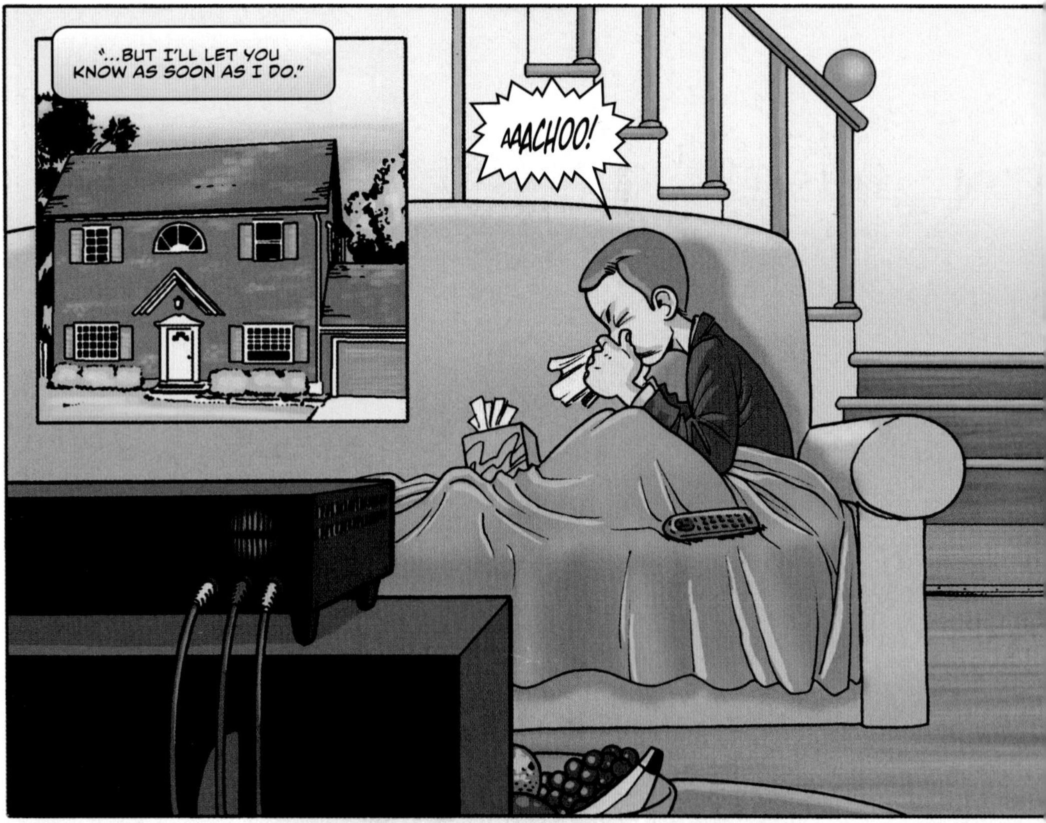
"...BUT I'LL LET YOU KNOW AS SOON AS I DO."
AAACHOO!
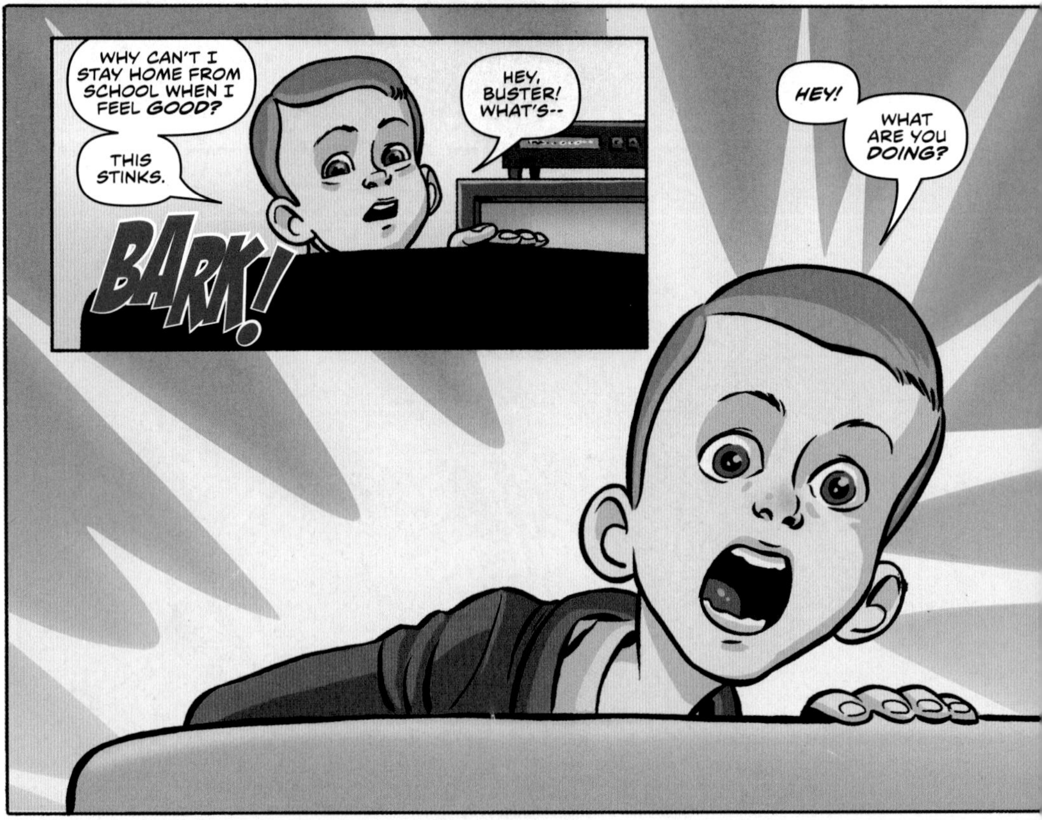
WHY CAN'T I STAY HOME FROM SCHOOL WHEN I FEEL *GOOD*?
THIS STINKS.
HEY, BUSTER! WHAT'S--
BARK!
HEY!
WHAT ARE YOU *DOING?*

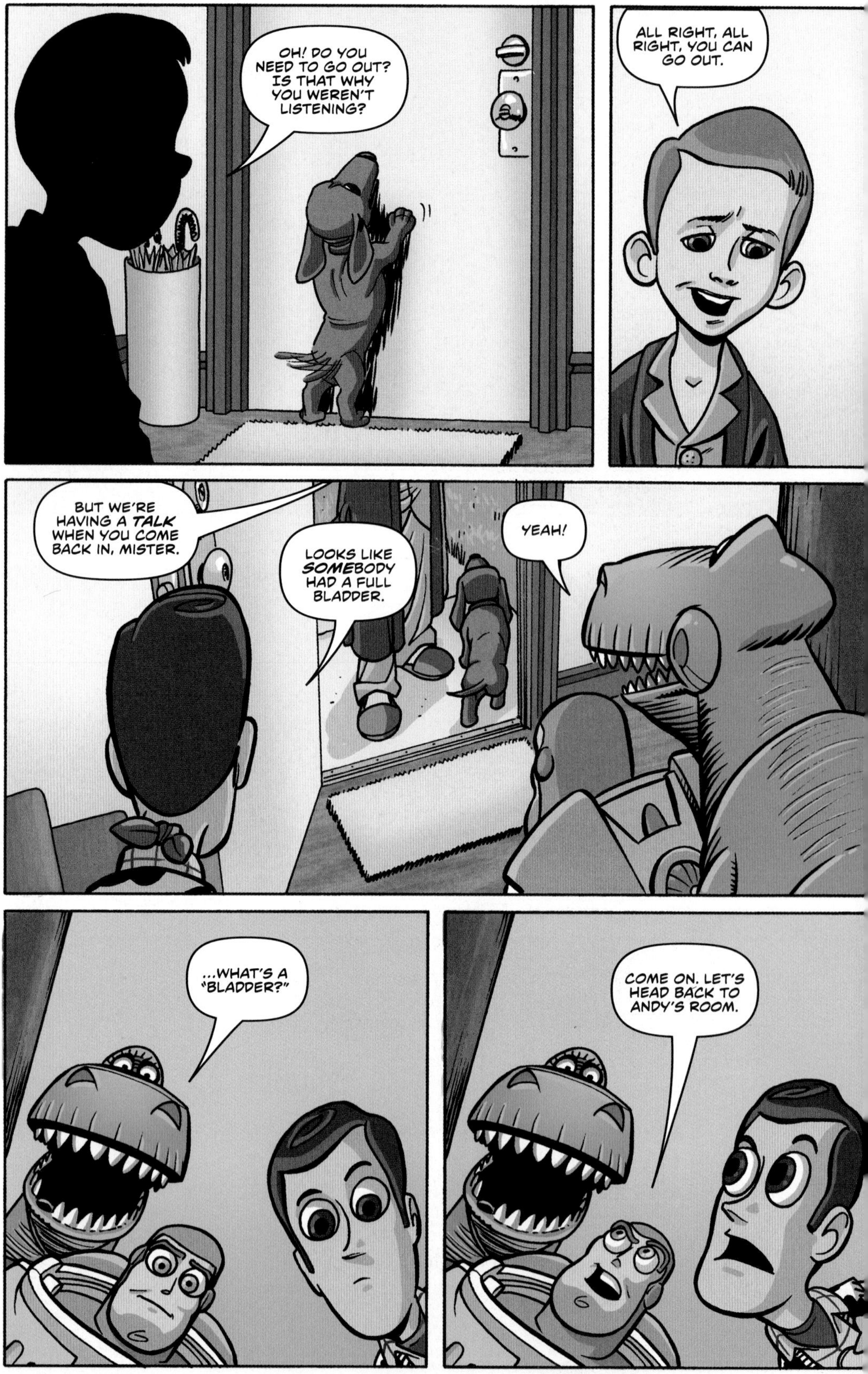
OH! DO YOU NEED TO GO OUT? IS THAT WHY YOU WEREN'T LISTENING?
ALL RIGHT, ALL RIGHT, YOU CAN GO OUT.
BUT WE'RE HAVING A *TALK* WHEN YOU COME BACK IN, MISTER.
LOOKS LIKE *SOME*BODY HAD A FULL BLADDER.
YEAH!
...WHAT'S A "BLADDER?"
COME ON. LET'S HEAD BACK TO ANDY'S ROOM.

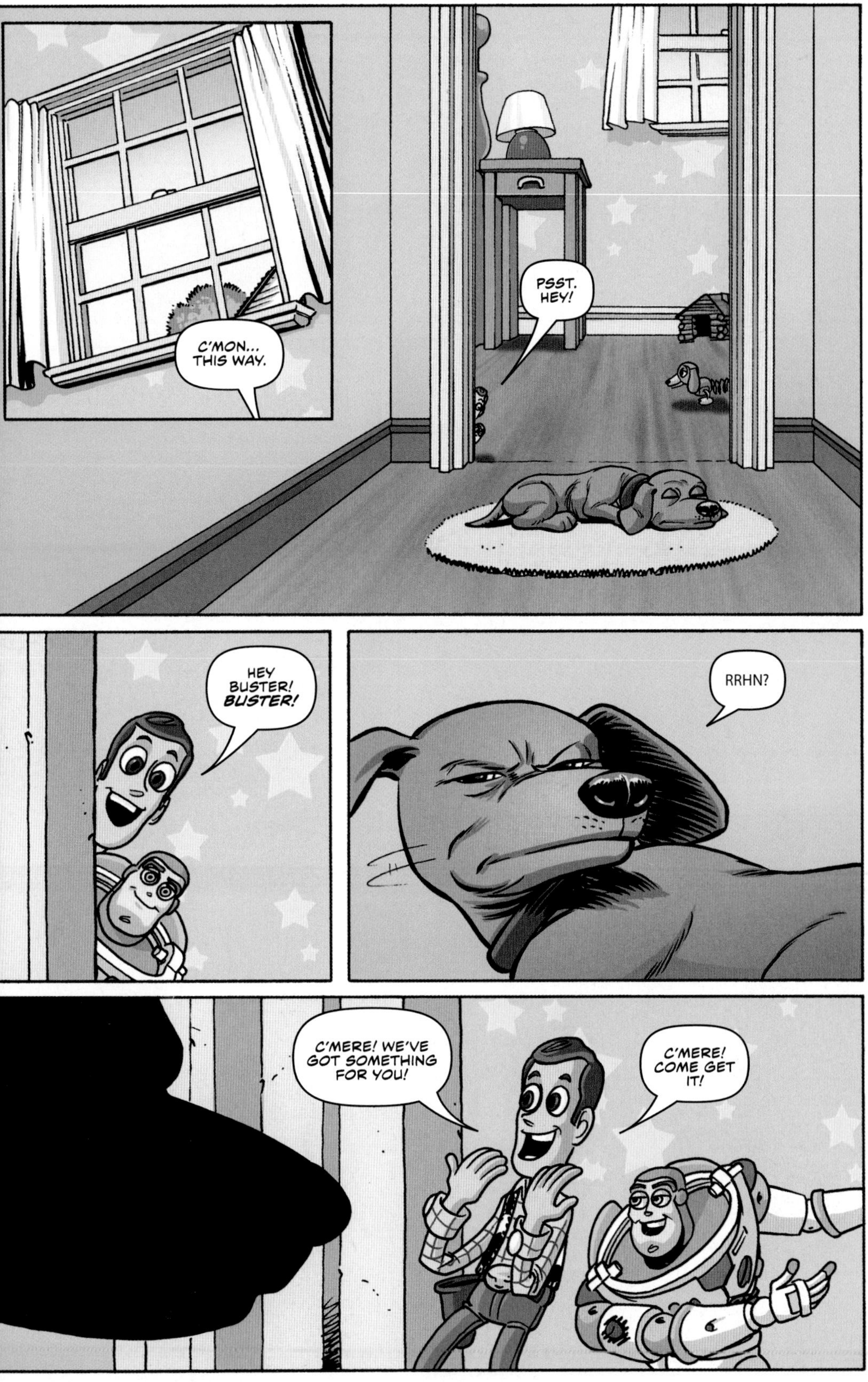
C'MON... THIS WAY.
PSST. HEY!
HEY BUSTER! BUSTER!
RRHN?
C'MERE! WE'VE GOT SOMETHING FOR YOU!
C'MERE! COME GET IT!

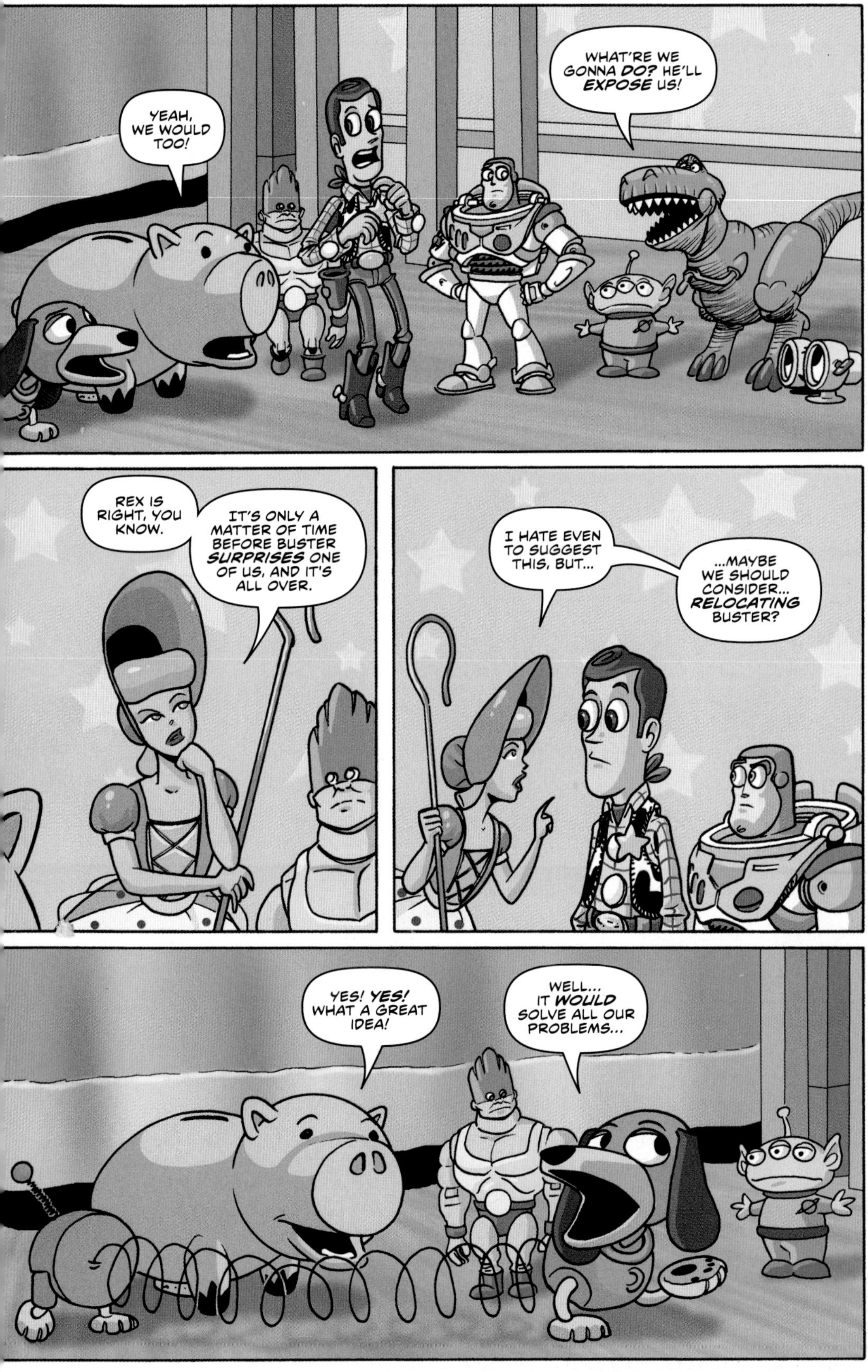
YEAH, WE WOULD TOO!
WHAT'RE WE GONNA DO? HE'LL EXPOSE US!
REX IS RIGHT, YOU KNOW.
IT'S ONLY A MATTER OF TIME BEFORE BUSTER SURPRISES ONE OF US, AND IT'S ALL OVER.
I HATE EVEN TO SUGGEST THIS, BUT...
...MAYBE WE SHOULD CONSIDER... RELOCATING BUSTER?
YES! YES! WHAT A GREAT IDEA!
WELL... IT WOULD SOLVE ALL OUR PROBLEMS...

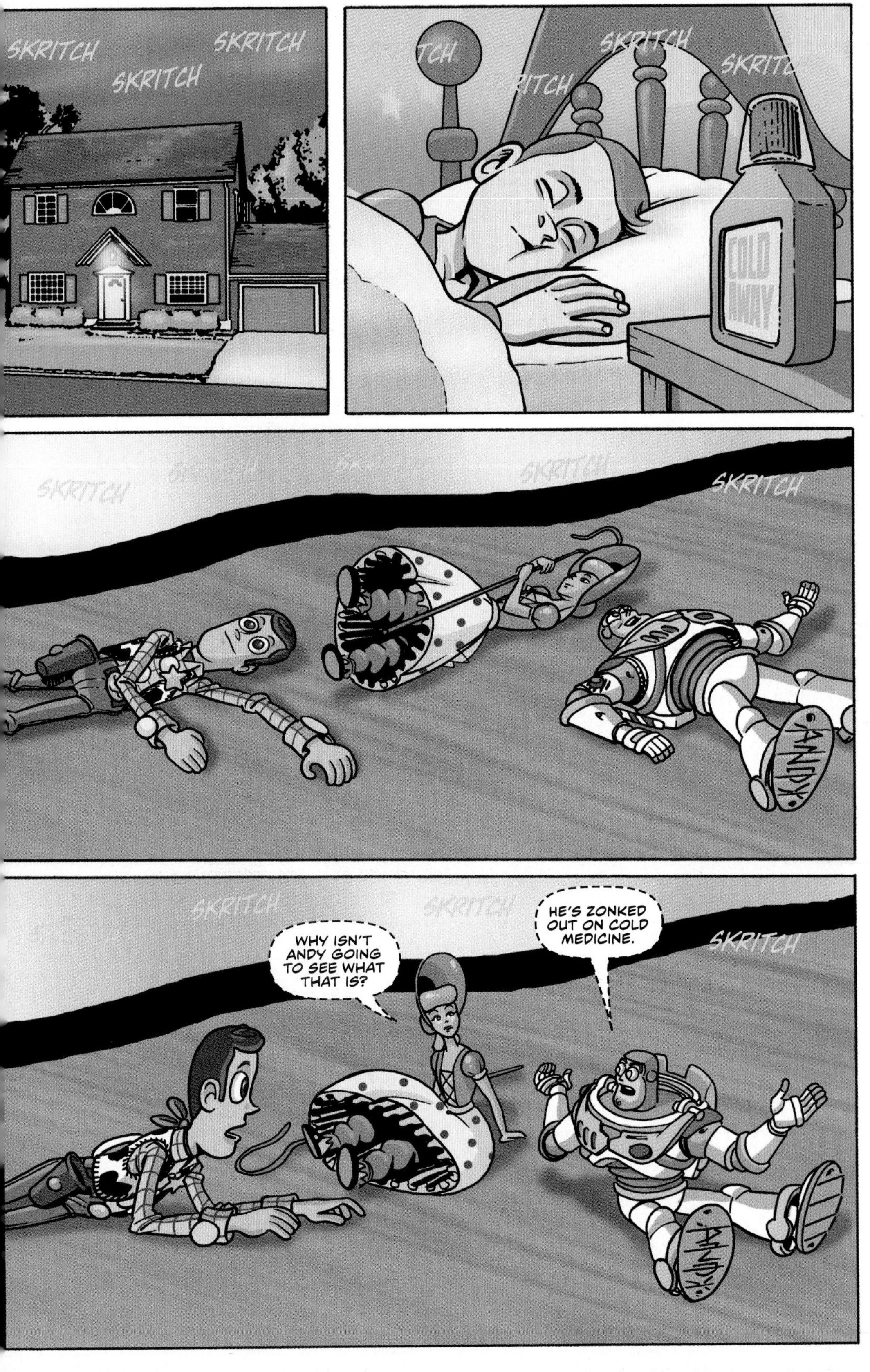
SKRITCH
SKRITCH
SKRITCH
SKRITCH
SKRITCH
COLD AWAY
SKRITCH
SKRITCH
SKRITCH
ANDY
SKRITCH
SKRITCH
WHY ISN'T ANDY GOING TO SEE WHAT THAT IS?
HE'S ZONKED OUT ON COLD MEDICINE.
SKRITCH
ANDY

CHAPTER FOUR

No Time for Sergeants

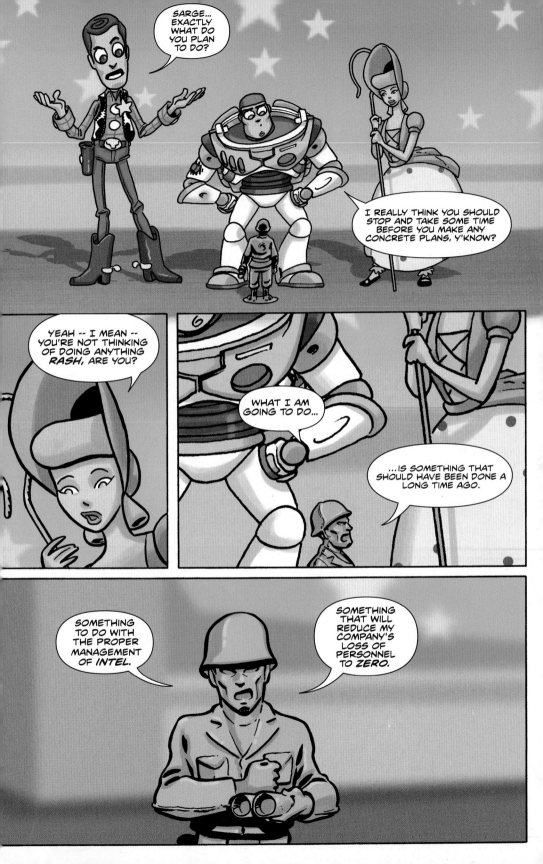

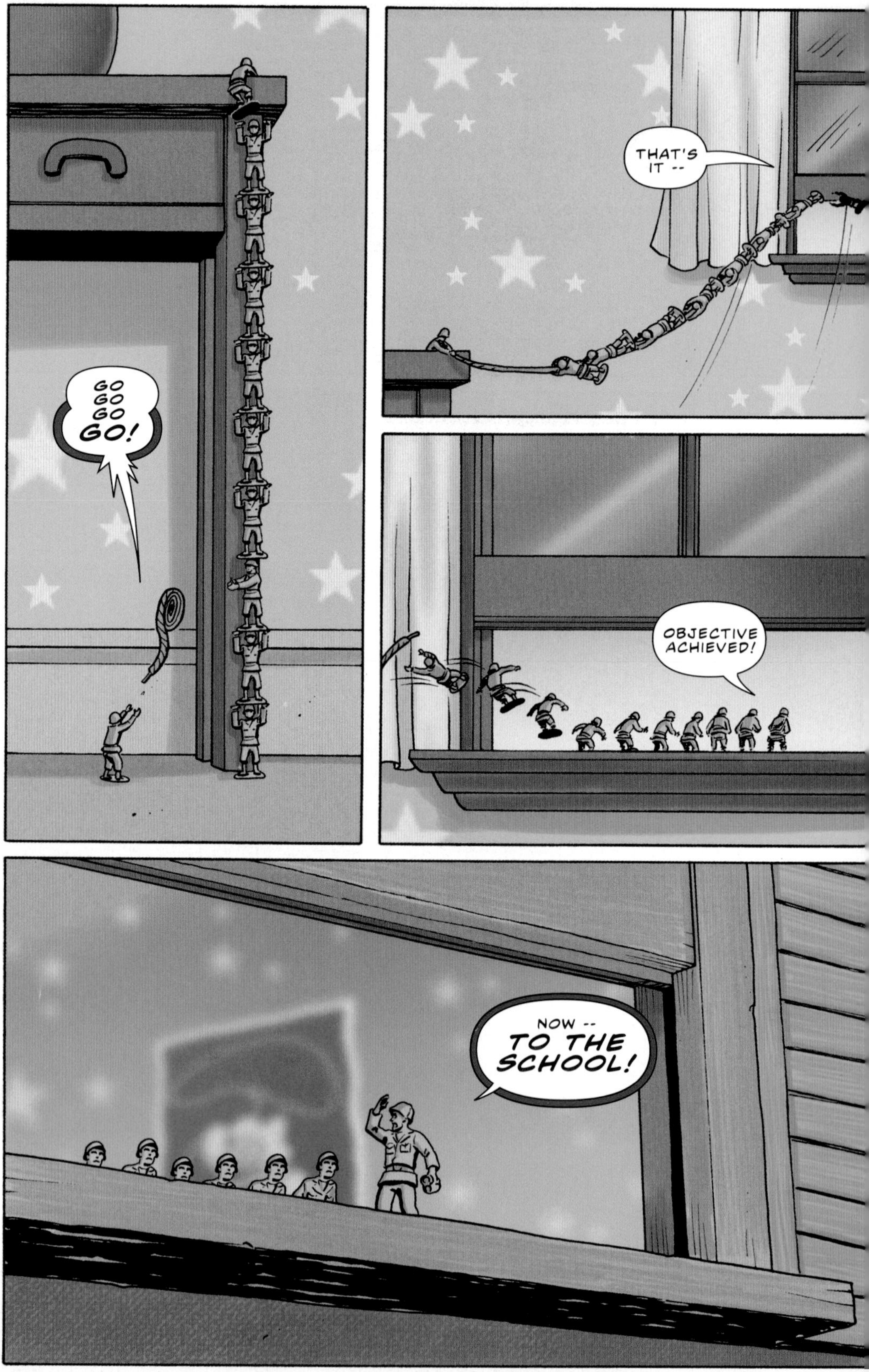
GO GO GO GO!
THAT'S IT --
OBJECTIVE ACHIEVED!
NOW -- TO THE SCHOOL!

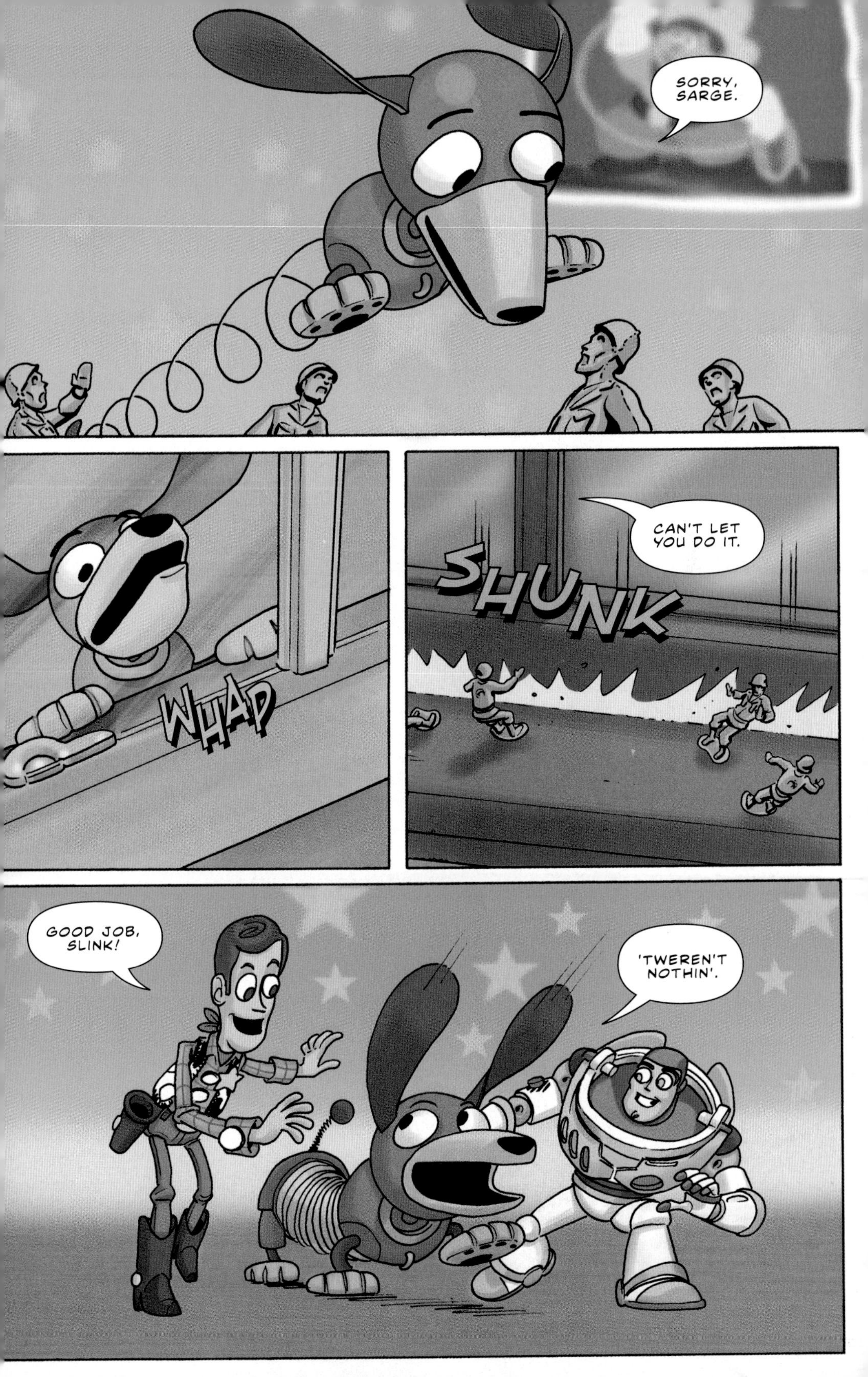
SORRY, SARGE.
WHAP
CAN'T LET YOU DO IT.
SHUNK
GOOD JOB, SLINK!
'TWEREN'T NOTHIN'.

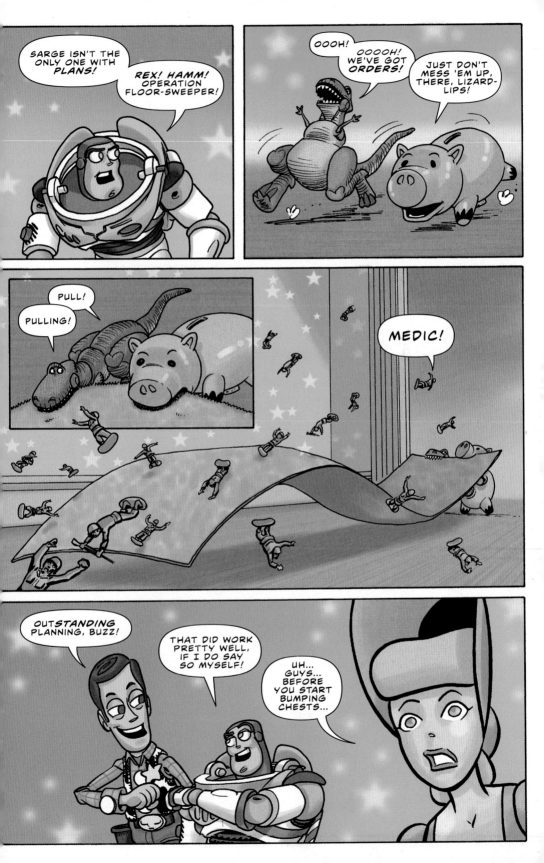

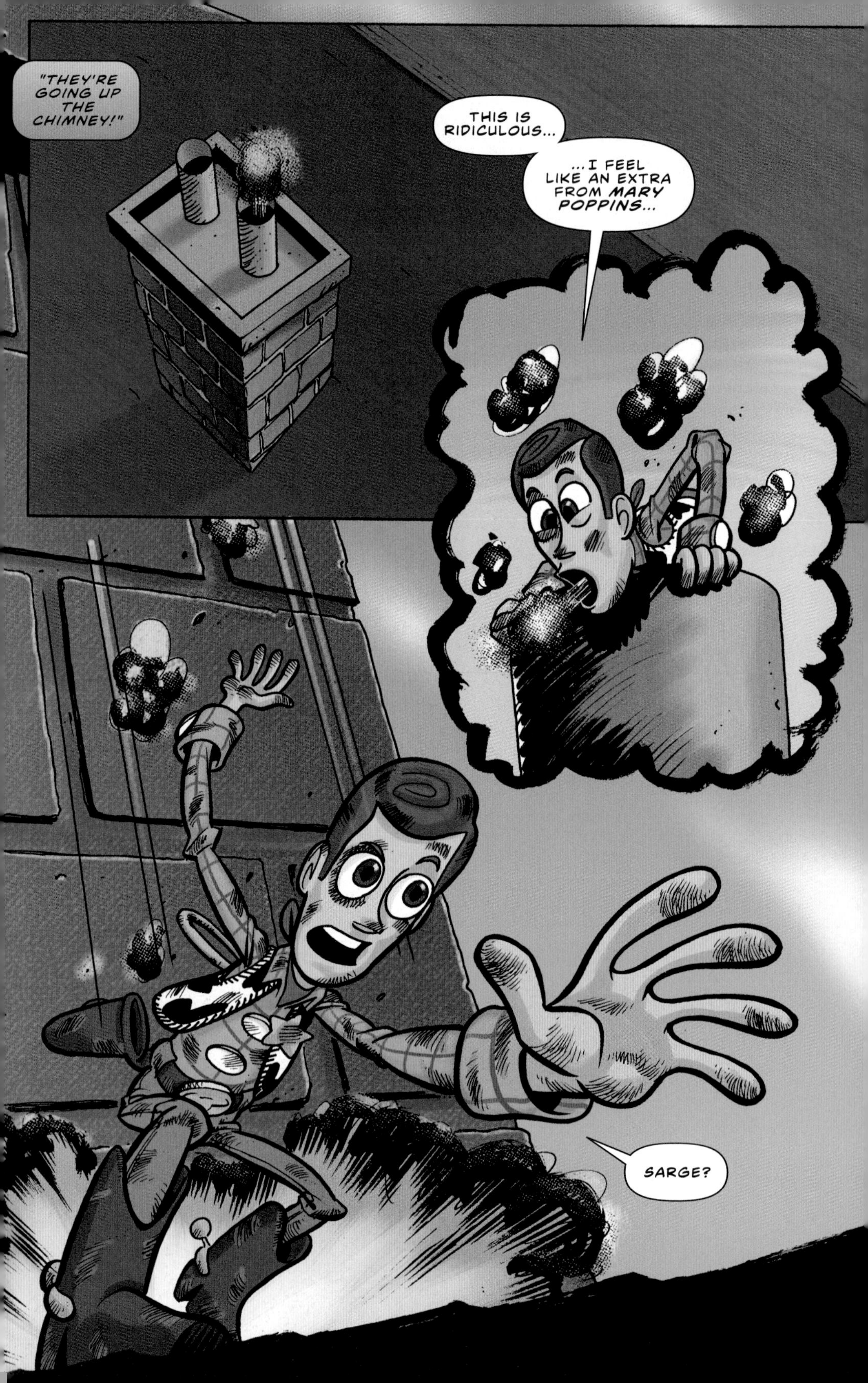
"THEY'RE GOING UP THE CHIMNEY!"
THIS IS RIDICULOUS...
...I FEEL LIKE AN EXTRA FROM *MARY POPPINS*...
SARGE?

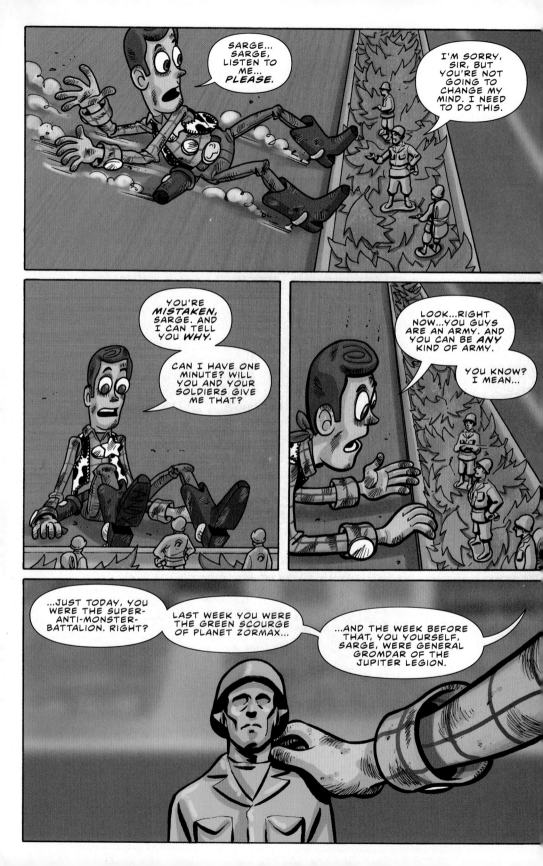

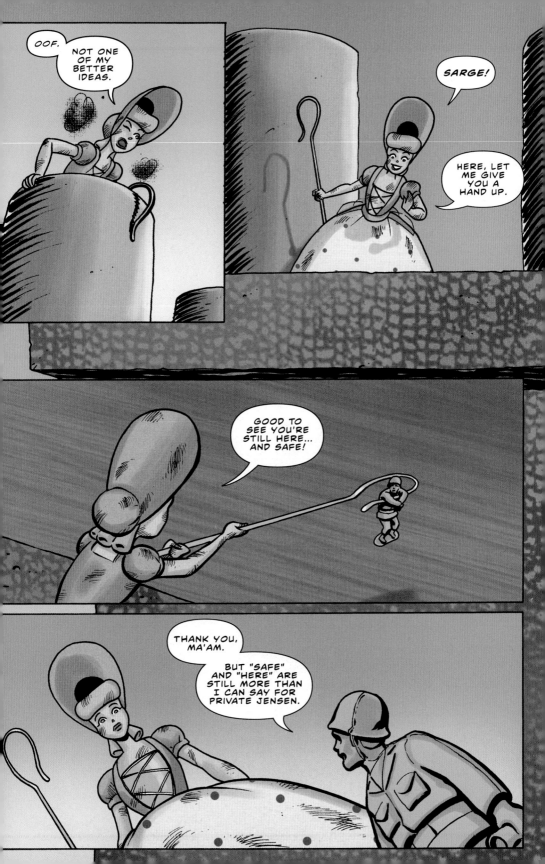

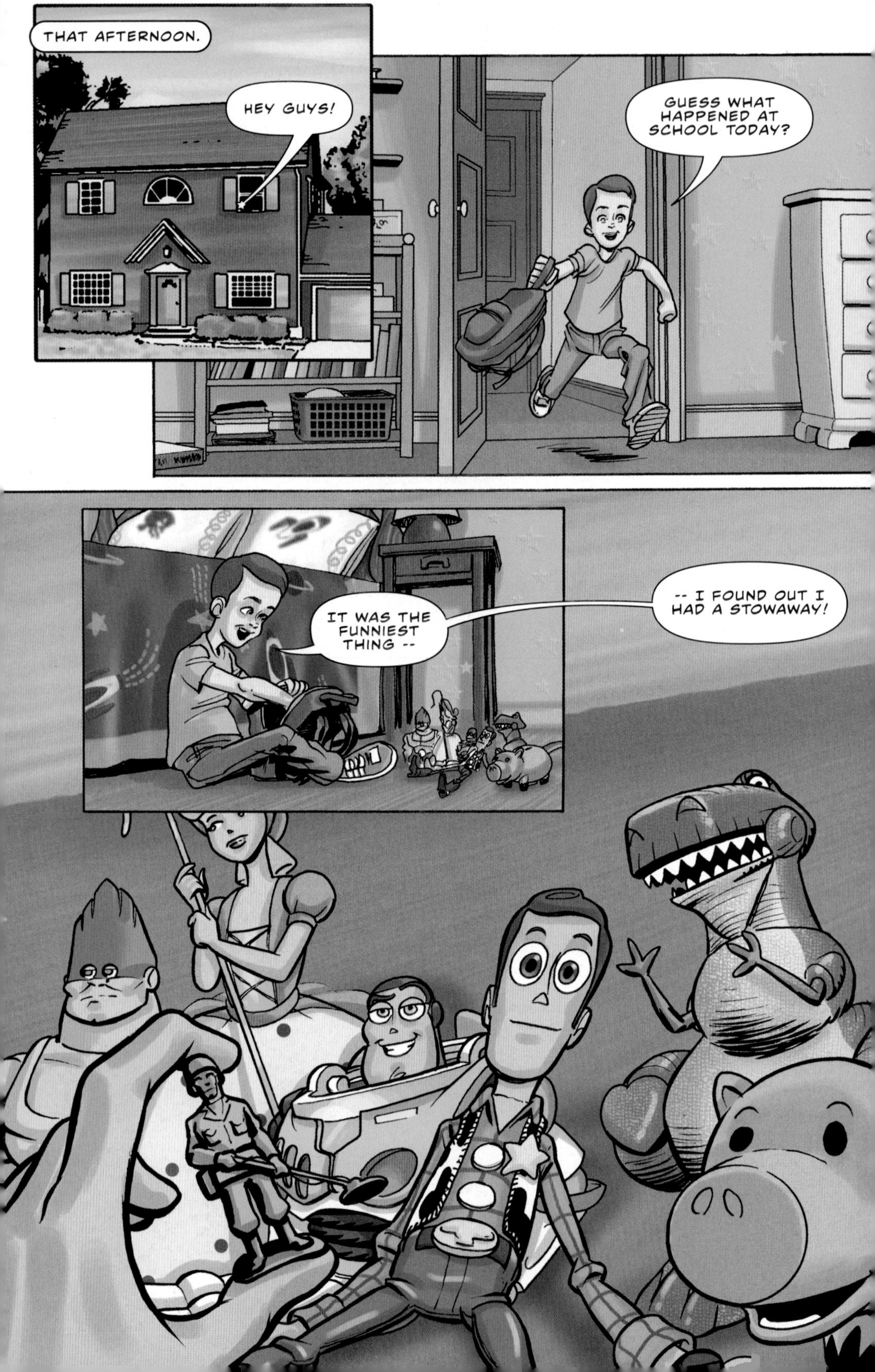
THAT AFTERNOON.
HEY GUYS!
GUESS WHAT HAPPENED AT SCHOOL TODAY?
IT WAS THE FUNNIEST THING --
-- I FOUND OUT I HAD A STOWAWAY!

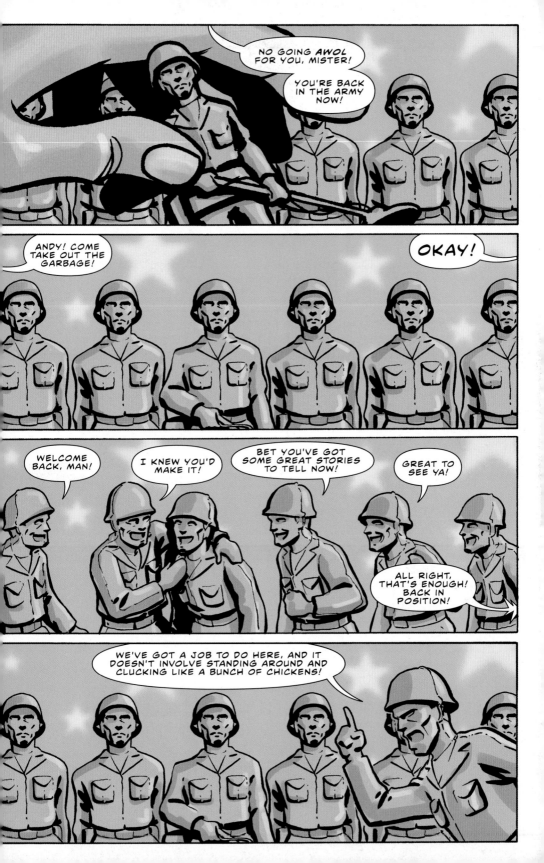

COVER GALLERY

ISSUE ONE

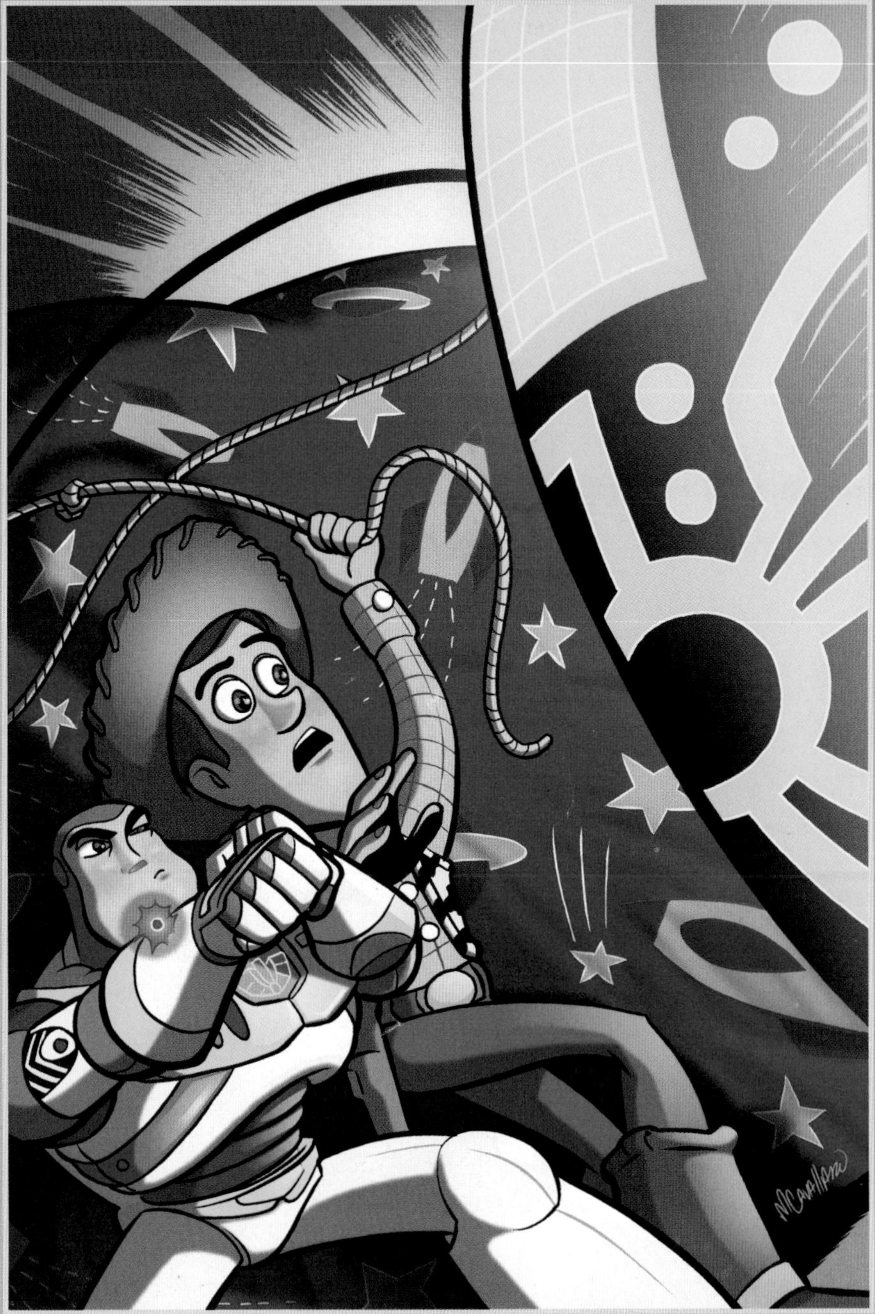

COVER A: MICHAEL CAVALLARO

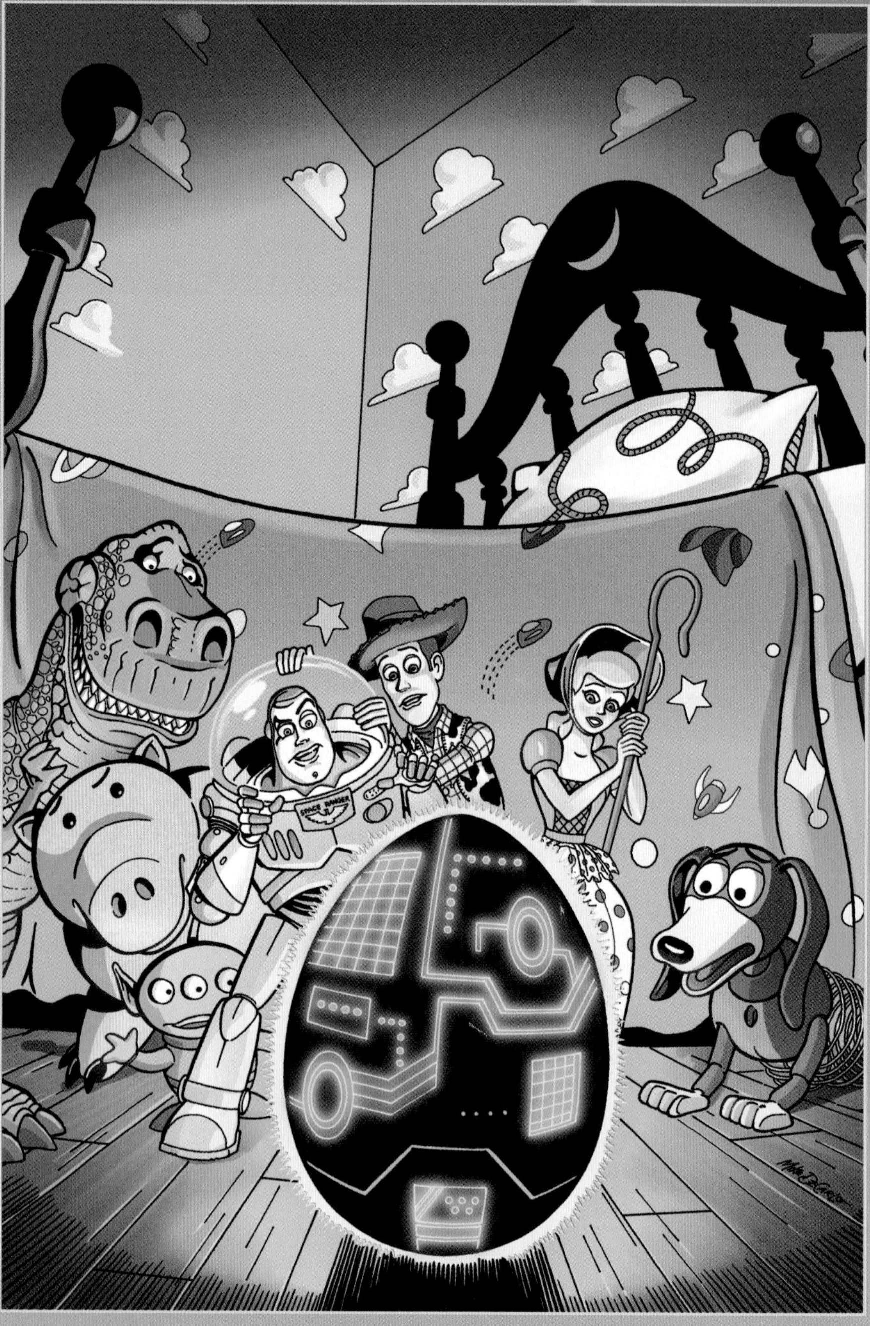
SPACE RANGER
Mike DeCarlo

COVER B: MIKE DECARLO

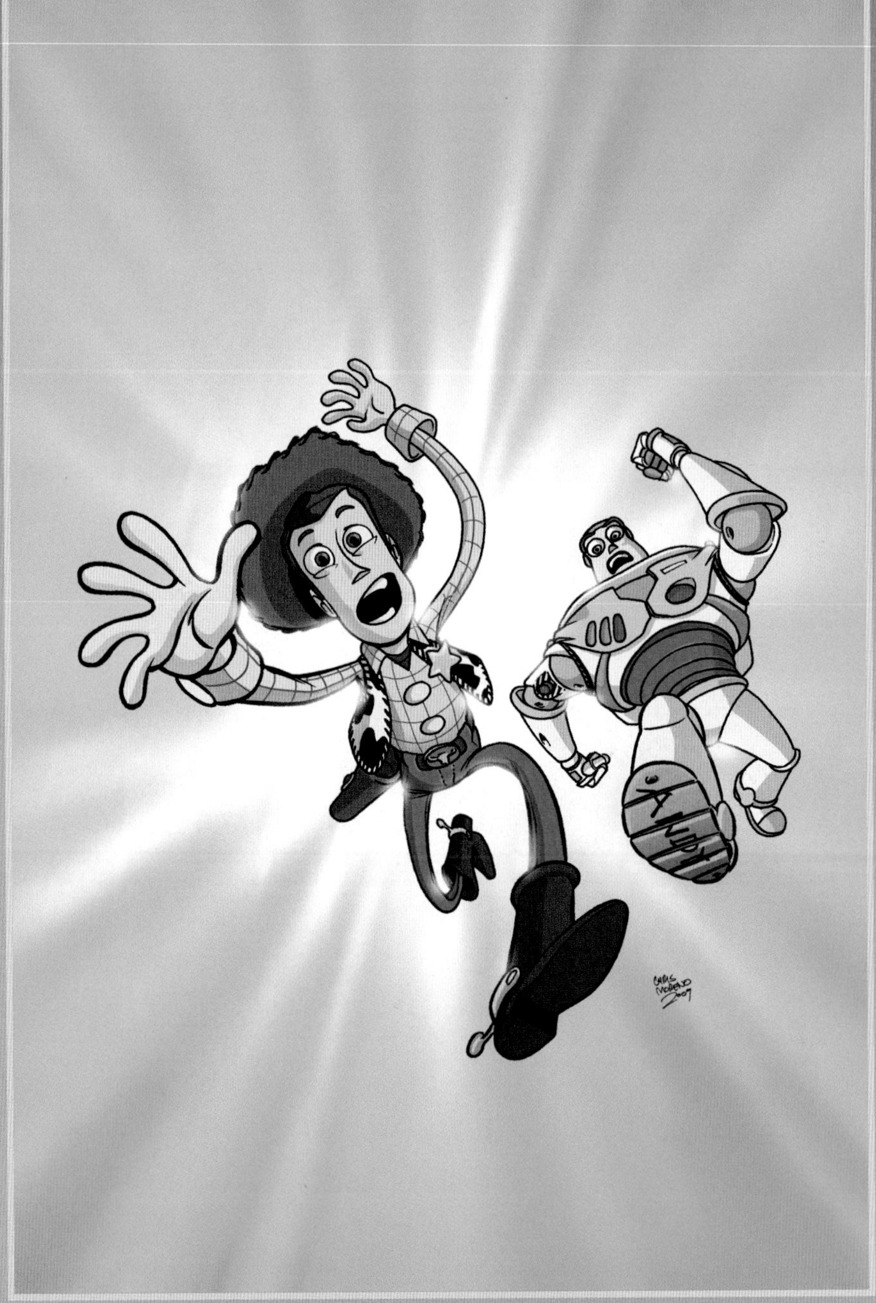

COVER C: CHRIS MORENO

RETAIL VARIANT: PHOTOCOVER

Issue Two

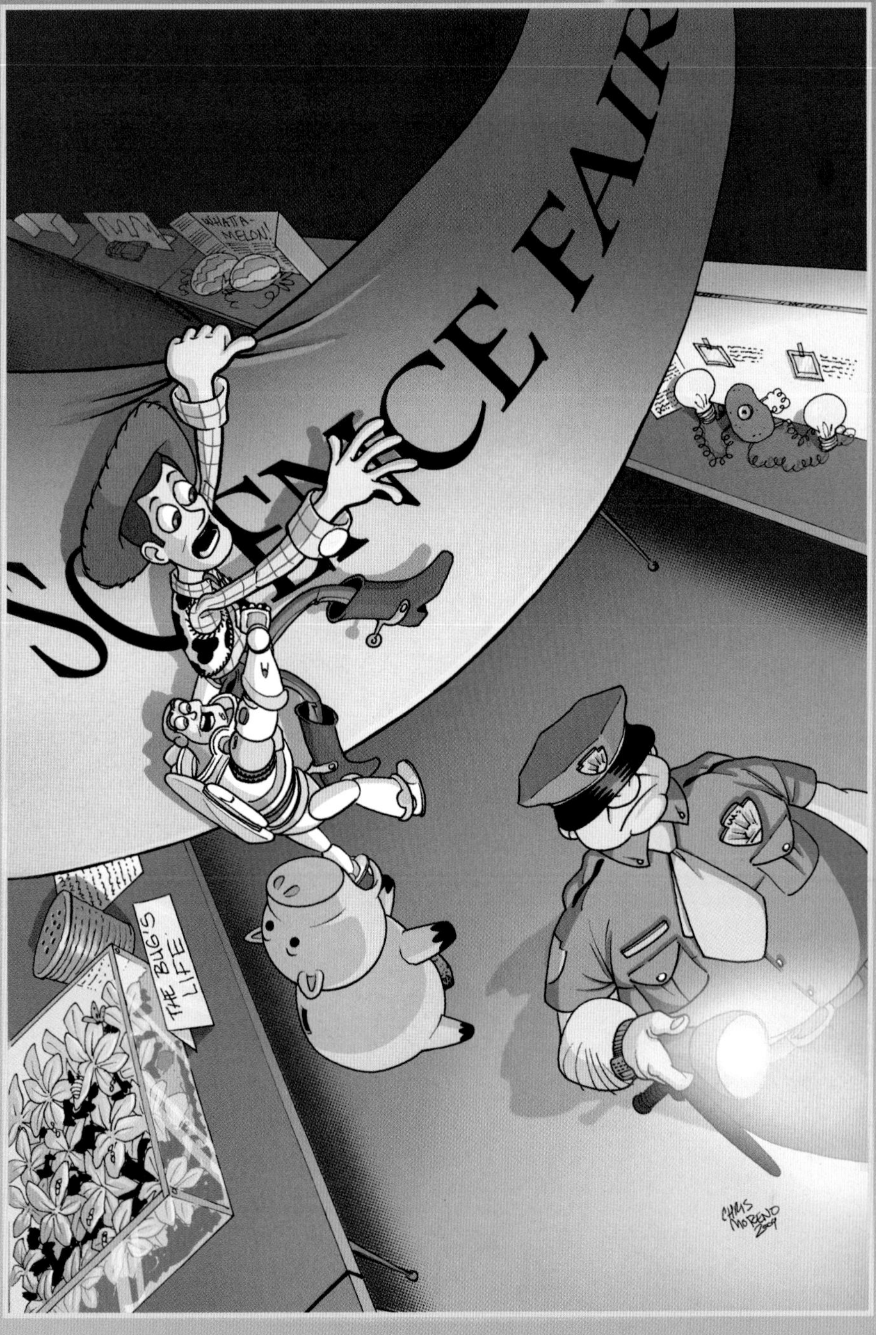

SCIENCE FAIR
WHATTA-MELON!
THE BUG'S LIFE
CHRIS MORENO 2009

Cover A: Chris Moreno

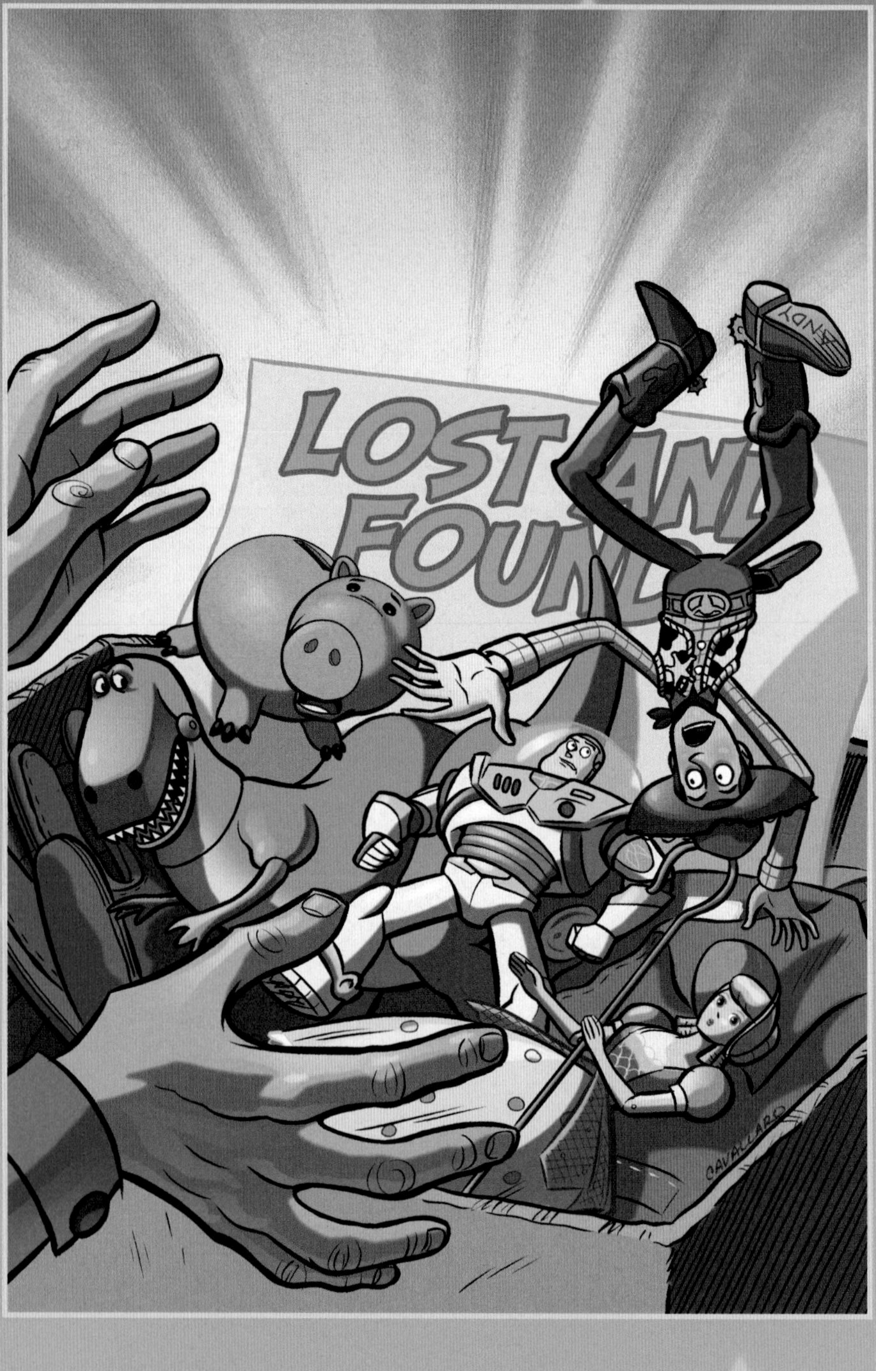
LOST AND FOUND
ANDY
CAVALLARO

Cover B: Michael Cavallero

RETAIL VARIANT: PHOTOCOVER

Issue Three

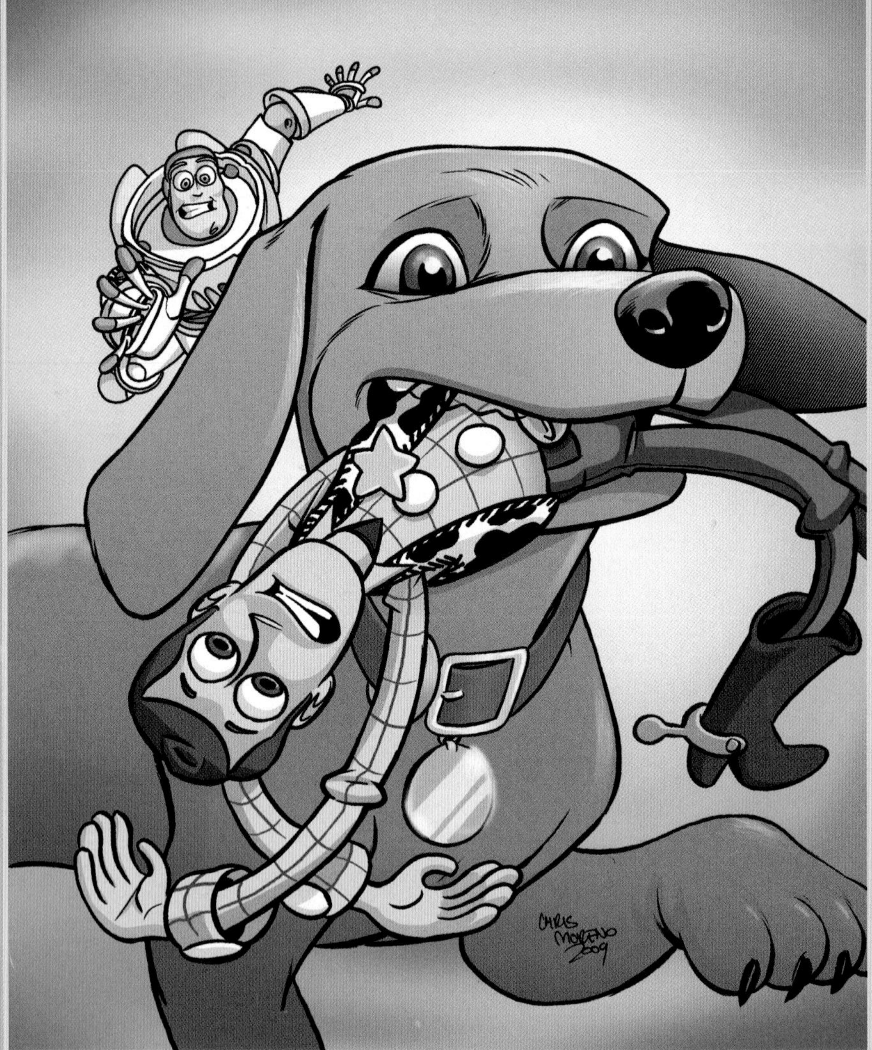
CHRIS MORENO 2009

Cover A: Chris Moreno

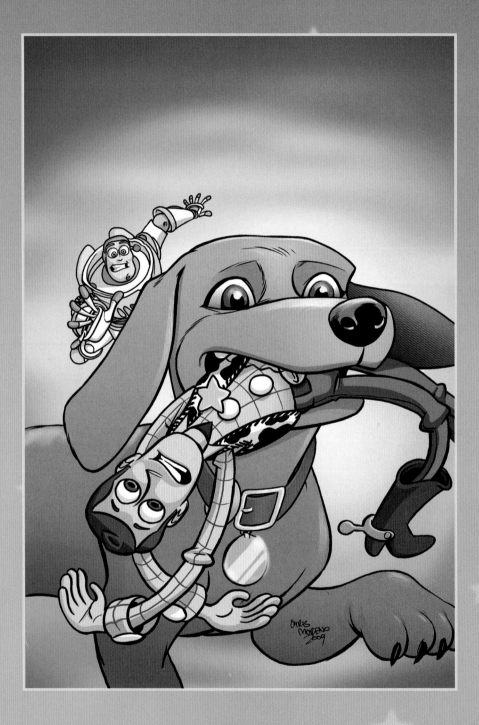

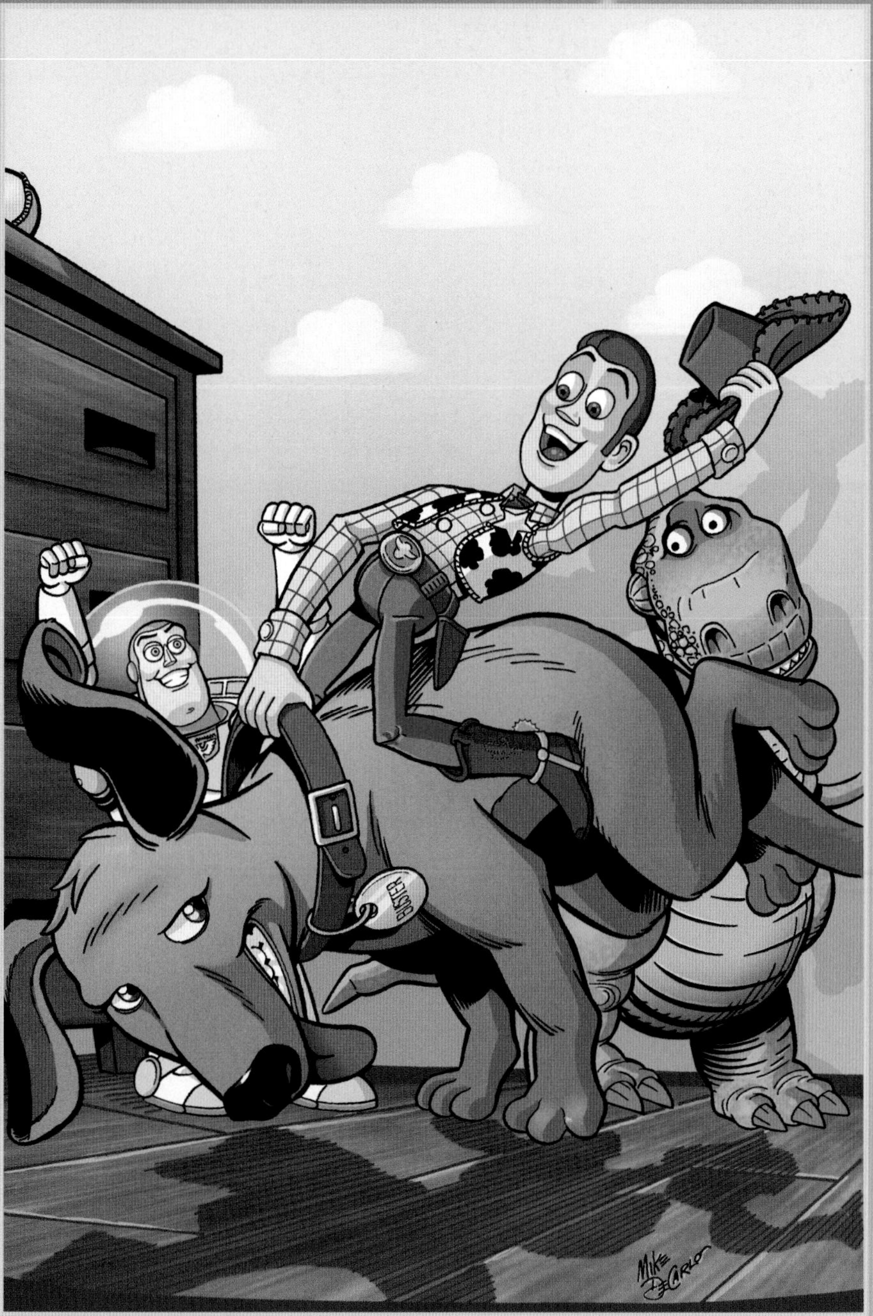
BUSTER
MIKE DECARLO

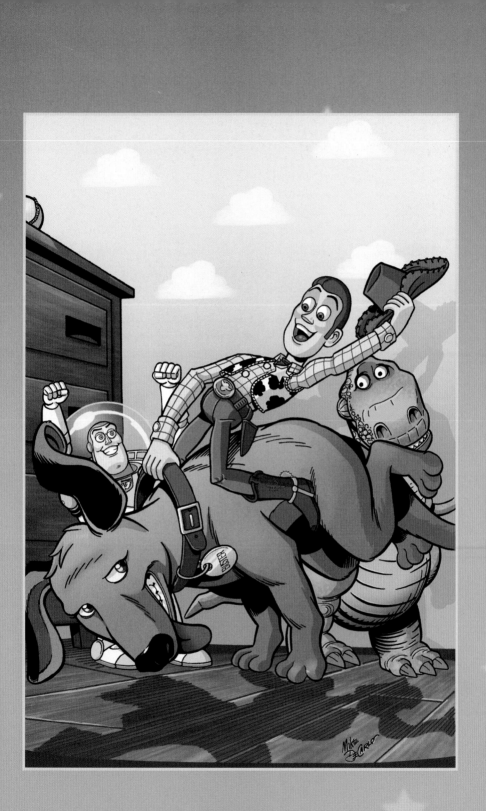

COVER B: MIKE DECARLO

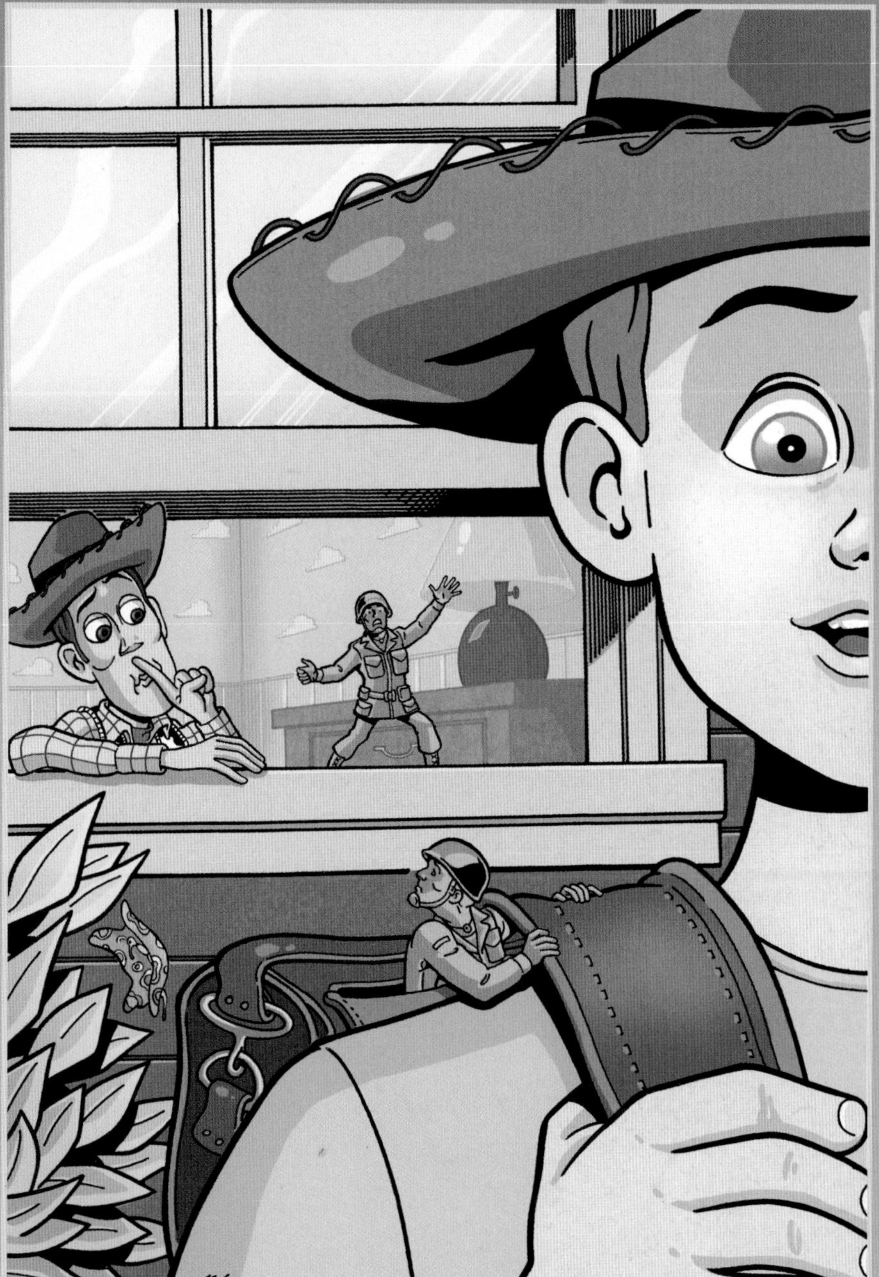
MIKE DECARLO

COVER B: MIKE DECARLO

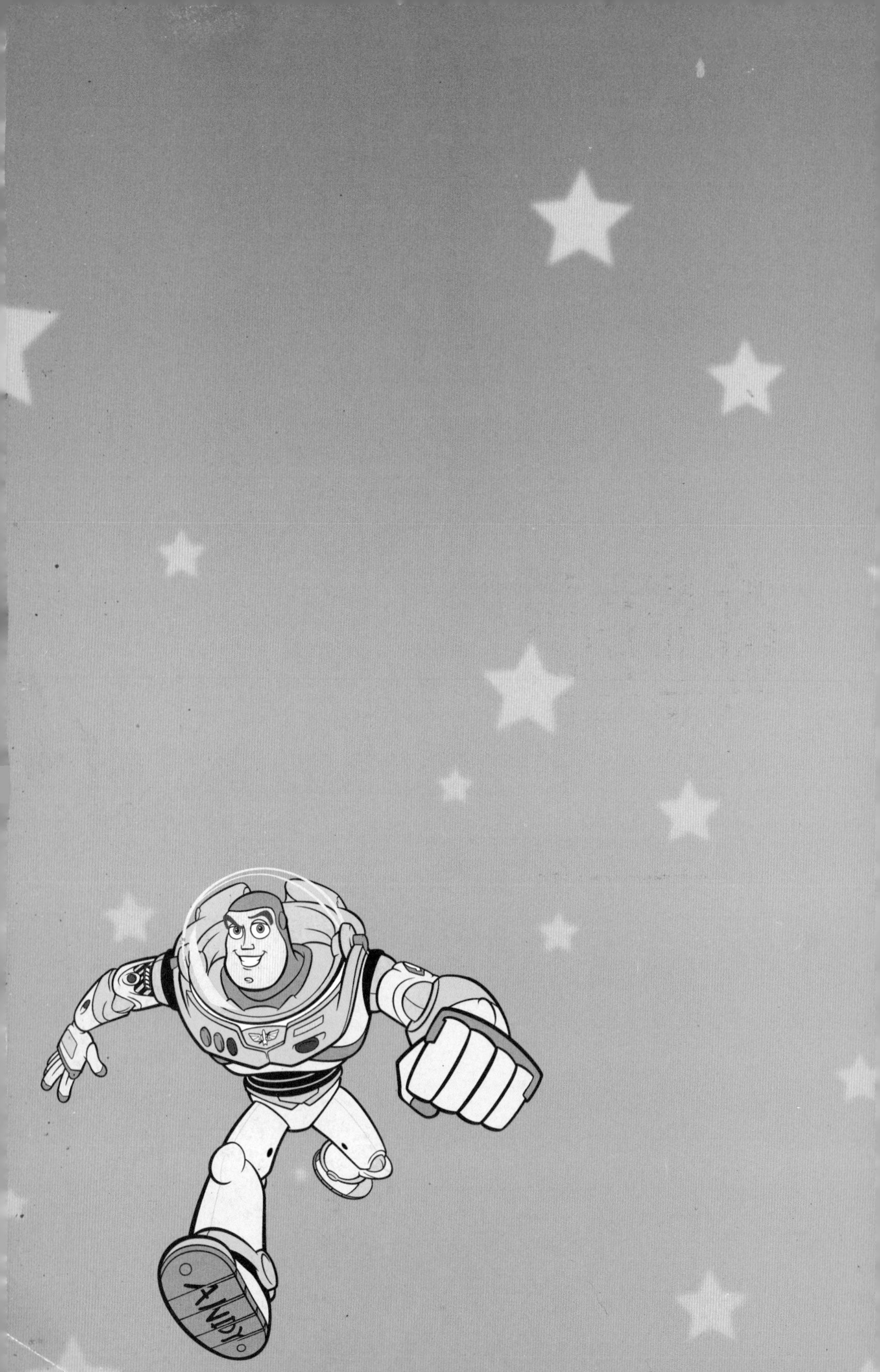
ANDY